knitting
goes
large

knitting goes large

Over 20 Designs from Rowan for Plus Sizes

SHARON BRANT

with
JENNIE ATKINSON
WENDY BAKER
KIM HARGREAVES
MARTIN STOREY

photography by
JOHN HESELTINE

R O W A N

KNITTING GOES LARGE

First published in 2008 by
Rowan Yarns
Green Lane Mill
Holmfirth
West Yorkshire
HD9 2DX

Editor Sally Harding
Designer Anne Wilson
Photographer John Heseltine
Styling Louise Sykes and Susan Berry
Pattern writer Sue Whiting
Pattern checker Emma King
Diagrams Lisa Richardson

Associate Publisher Susan Berry

Brtish Library Cataloguing in Publication Data
A catalogue record of this book is available
from the British Library

ISBN 978-1-906007-43-0

Reproduced in Singaore and printed in China

projects

cabled tunic

MARTIN STOREY

97	102	107	112	117	122	cm
38	40	42	44	46	48	in

FINISHED MEASUREMENTS

Around bust

117	123	128	133	138	143	cm
46	48½	50½	52¼	54¼	56¼	in

Length to shoulder

70	71	72	73	74	75	cm
27½	28	28¼	28¾	29	29½	in

Sleeve seam

44	44	45	45	45	45	cm
17¼	17¼	17¾	17¾	17¾	17¾	in

YARN

23 (24: 25: 26: 27: 28) x 50g/1¾oz balls of Rowan *Denim* in Memphis 229

NEEDLES

Pair of 3¼mm (UK no 10) (US size 3) knitting needles
Pair of 4mm (UK no 8) (US size 6) knitting needles

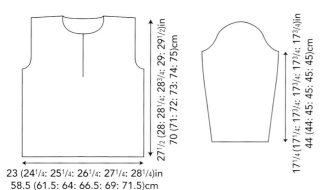

23 (24¼: 25¼: 26¼: 27¼: 28¼)in
58.5 (61.5: 64: 66.5: 69: 71.5)cm

27½ (28: 28¼: 28¾: 29: 29½)in
70 (71: 72: 73: 74: 75)cm

17¼ (17¼: 17¾: 17¾: 17¾: 17¾)in
44 (44: 45: 45: 45: 45)cm

3¼mm (UK no 10) (US size 3) circular knitting needle
Cable needle

TENSION

Before washing: 23 sts and 28 rows to 10cm/4in measured over patt using 4mm (US size 6) needles *or size to obtain correct tension.*

SPECIAL NOTE

Rowan *Denim* shrinks in length when washed for the first time. Allowances have been made in the pattern for this shrinkage. The finished measurements given are those obtained after washing.

ABBREVIATIONS

See page 132.

SPECIAL ABBREVIATIONS

Tw2R = slip next st onto cable needle and leave at back of work, K1 tbl, then P1 from cable needle; **Tw2L** = slip next st onto cable needle and leave at front of work, P1, then K1 tbl from cable needle; **C3B** = slip next 2 sts onto cable needle and leave at back of work, K1, then K2 from cable needle; **C3F** = slip next st onto cable needle and leave at front of work, K2, then K1 from cable needle; **Cr3L** = slip next st onto cable needle and leave at front of work, K1 tbl, P1, then K1 tbl from cable needle.

BACK

Using 3¼mm (US size 3) needles, cast on 117 (123: 129: 135: 141: 147) sts.
Row 1 (RS) K1, *P1, K1; rep from * to end.
Row 2 As row 1.

These 2 rows form moss st.

Work in moss st for 7 rows more, ending with WS facing for next row.

Row 10 (WS) Moss st 27 (30: 33: 36: 39: 42) sts, *[M1, moss st 3 sts] twice, [M1, moss st 2 sts] 4 times, [M1, moss st 3 sts] twice, M1*, moss st 23 sts; rep from * to * once more, moss st to end. 135 (141: 147: 153: 159: 165) sts.

Change to 4mm (US size 6) needles.

Now work in cable patt as follows:

Row 1 (RS) Moss st 26 (29: 32: 35: 38: 41) sts, *[P1, K1 tbl] twice, P3, K1 tbl, P1, K1 tbl, P2, K7, P2, K1 tbl, P1, K1 tbl, P3, [K1 tbl, P1] twice*, moss st 21 sts; rep from * to * once more, moss st to end.

Row 2 Moss st 26 (29: 32: 35: 38: 41) sts, *[K1, P1 tbl] twice, K3, P1 tbl, K1, P1 tbl, K2, P7, K2, P1 tbl, K1, P1 tbl, K3, [P1 tbl, K1] twice*, moss st 21 sts; rep from * to * once more, moss st to end.

Row 3 Moss st 26 (29: 32: 35: 38: 41) sts, *[P1, K1 tbl] twice, P3, K1 tbl, P1, K1 tbl, P2, C3B, K1, C3F, P2, K1 tbl, P1, K1 tbl, P3, [K1 tbl, P1] twice*, moss st 21 sts; rep from * to * once more, moss st to end.

Row 4 As row 2.

Row 5 Moss st 26 (29: 32: 35: 38: 41) sts, *P1, K1 tbl, P1, Tw2L, P1, Tw2R, P1, K1 tbl, P2, K7, P2, K1 tbl, P1, Tw2L, P1, Tw2R, P1, K1 tbl, P1*, moss st 21 sts; rep from * to * once more, moss st to end.

Row 6 Moss st 26 (29: 32: 35: 38: 41) sts, *K1, P1 tbl, K2, P1 tbl, K1, [P1 tbl, K2] twice, P7, [K2, P1 tbl] twice, K1, P1 tbl, K2, P1 tbl, K1*, moss st 21 sts; rep from * to * once more, moss st to end.

Row 7 Moss st 26 (29: 32: 35: 38: 41) sts, *P1, K1 tbl, P2, Cr3L, P2, K1 tbl, P2, C3B, K1, C3F, P2, K1 tbl, P2, Cr3L, P2, K1 tbl, P1*, moss st 21 sts; rep from * to * once more, moss st to end.

Row 8 As row 6.

Row 9 Moss st 26 (29: 32: 35: 38: 41) sts, *P1, K1 tbl, P1, Tw2R, P1, Tw2L, P1, K1 tbl, P2, K7, P2, K1 tbl, P1, Tw2R, P1, Tw2L, P1, K1 tbl, P1*, moss st 21 sts; rep from * to * once more, moss st to end.

Row 10 As row 2.

Row 11 As row 3.

Row 12 As row 2.

These 12 rows form patt.**

Work straight in patt until Back measures 56 (56: 57: 57:

58.5: 58.5)cm/22 (22: 22½: 22½: 23: 23)in from cast-on edge, ending with RS facing for next row.

Shape armholes

Keeping patt correct, cast off 8 (8: 9: 9: 10: 10) sts at beg of next 2 rows. 119 (125: 129: 135: 139: 145) sts.

Dec 1 st at each end of next 5 (7: 7: 9: 9: 11) rows, then on foll 3 (3: 4: 4: 5: 5) alt rows, then on 2 foll 4th rows. 99 (101: 103: 105: 107: 109) sts.

Work straight until armhole measures 25.5 (27: 27: 28: 28: 29)cm/10 (10½: 10½: 11: 11: 11½)in, ending with RS facing for next row.

Shape back neck and shoulders

Cast off 9 (10: 10: 10: 10: 11) sts at beg of next 2 rows. 81 (81: 83: 85: 87: 87) sts.

Next row (RS) Cast off 9 (10: 10: 10: 10: 11) sts, patt until there are 14 (13: 14: 14: 15: 14) sts on right needle and turn, leaving rem sts on a holder.

Work each side of neck separately.

Cast off 4 sts at beg of next row.

Cast off rem 10 (9: 10: 10: 11: 10) sts.

With RS facing, rejoin yarn to rem sts, cast off centre 35 (35: 35: 37: 37: 37) sts, patt to end.

Complete to match first side, reversing shapings.

POCKET LININGS (make 2)

Using 4mm (US size 6) needles, cast on 29 sts.

Starting with a K row, work in st st for 49 rows, ending with WS facing for next row.

Row 50 (WS) P4, [M1, P3] 7 times, M1, P4. 37 sts.

Break off yarn and leave sts on a holder.

FRONT

Work as given for Back to **.

Work in patt for 42 rows more, ending with RS facing for next row.

Place pockets

Next row (RS) Patt 20 (23: 26: 29: 32: 35) sts, slip next 37 sts onto a holder and, in their place, patt across 37 sts of first Pocket Lining, patt 21 sts, slip next 37 sts onto a holder and, in their place, patt across 37 sts of second Pocket Lining, patt to end.

Work straight until 9 rows fewer have been worked than on Back to start of armhole shaping, ending with WS facing for next row.

Next row (WS) Patt 67 (70: 73: 76: 79: 82) sts, inc in next st, patt to end. 136 (142: 148: 154: 160: 166) sts.

Divide for front opening

Next row (RS) Patt 68 (71: 74: 77: 80: 83) sts and turn, leaving rem sts on a holder.

Work each side of neck separately.

Work 7 rows, ending with RS facing for next row.

Shape armhole

Keeping patt correct, cast off 8 (8: 9: 9: 10: 10) sts at beg of next row. 60 (63: 65: 68: 70: 73) sts.

Work 1 row.

Dec 1 st at armhole edge of next 5 (7: 7: 9: 9: 11) rows, then on foll 3 (3: 4: 4: 5: 5) alt rows, then on 2 foll 4th rows. 50 (51: 52: 53: 54: 55) sts.

Work straight until 21 rows fewer have been worked than on Back to start of shoulder shaping, ending with WS facing for next row.

Shape neck

Keeping patt correct, cast off 11 (11: 11: 12: 12: 12) sts at beg of next row. 39 (40: 41: 41: 42: 43) sts.

Dec 1 st at neck edge of next 5 rows, then on foll 5 alt rows, then on foll 4th row. 28 (29: 30: 30: 31: 32) sts.

Work 1 row, ending with RS facing for next row.

Shape shoulder

Cast off 9 (10: 10: 10: 10: 11) sts at beg of next row and foll alt row.

Work 1 row.

Cast off rem 10 (9: 10: 10: 11: 10) sts.

With RS facing, rejoin yarn to rem sts, patt to end.

Complete to match first side, reversing shapings.

SLEEVES (make 2)

Using 3¼mm (US size 3) needles, cast on 57 (57: 59: 61: 61: 63) sts.

Row 1 (RS) K0 (0: 1: 2: 2: 3), P3, *K3, P3; rep from * to last 0 (0: 1: 2: 2: 3) sts, K0 (0: 1: 2: 2: 3).

Row 2 P0 (0: 1: 2: 2: 3), K3, *P3, K3; rep from * to last 0 (0: 1: 2: 2: 3) sts, P0 (0: 1: 2: 2: 3).

These 2 rows form rib.

Work in rib for 13 rows more, ending with WS facing for next row.

Row 16 (WS) Rib 19 (19: 20: 21: 21: 22), [M1, rib 3] twice, [M1, rib 2] 4 times, [M1, rib 3] twice, M1, rib to last st, inc in last st. 67 (67: 69: 71: 71: 73) sts.

Change to 4mm (US size 6) needles.

Now work in cable patt as follows:

Row 1 (RS) P0 (0: 1: 0: 0: 1), [K1, P1] 9 (9: 9: 10: 10: 10) times, [P1, K1 tbl] twice, P3, K1 tbl, P1, K1 tbl, P2, K7, P2, K1 tbl, P1, K1 tbl, P3, [K1 tbl, P1] twice, [P1, K1] 9 (9: 9: 10: 10: 10) times, P0 (0: 1: 0: 0: 1).

Row 2 P0 (0: 1: 0: 0: 1), [K1, P1] 9 (9: 9: 10: 10: 10) times, [K1, P1 tbl] twice, K3, P1 tbl, K1, P1 tbl, K2, P7, K2, P1 tbl, K1, P1 tbl, K3, [P1 tbl, K1] twice, [P1, K1] 9 (9: 9: 10: 10: 10) times, P0 (0: 1: 0: 0: 1).

These 2 rows set position of moss st at sides of central cable panel.

Keeping moss st correct as now set, cont as follows:

Row 3 Moss st 18 (18: 19: 20: 20: 21) sts, [P1, K1 tbl] twice, P3, K1 tbl, P1, K1 tbl, P2, C3B, K1, C3F, P2, K1 tbl, P1, K1 tbl, P3, [K1 tbl, P1] twice, moss st to end.

Row 4 As row 2.

Row 5 Moss st 18 (18: 19: 20: 20: 21) sts, P1, K1 tbl, P1, Tw2L, P1, Tw2R, P1, K1 tbl, P2, K7, P2, K1 tbl, P1, Tw2L, P1, Tw2R, P1, K1 tbl, P1, moss st to end.

Row 6 Moss st 18 (18: 19: 20: 20: 21) sts, K1, P1 tbl, K2, P1 tbl, K1, [P1 tbl, K2] twice, P7, [K2, P1 tbl] twice, K1, P1 tbl, K2, P1 tbl, K1, moss st to end.

Row 7 Moss st 18 (18: 19: 20: 20: 21) sts, P1, K1 tbl, P2, Cr3L, P2, K1 tbl, P2, C3B, K1, C3F, P2, K1 tbl, P2, Cr3L, P2, K1 tbl, P1, moss st to end.

Row 8 As row 6.

Row 9 [Inc in first st] 0 (0: 0: 0: 1: 1) times, moss st 18 (18: 19: 20: 19: 20) sts, P1, K1 tbl, P1, Tw2R, P1, Tw2L, P1, K1 tbl, P2, K7, P2, K1 tbl, P1, Tw2R, P1, Tw2L, P1, K1 tbl, P1, moss st to last 0 (0: 0: 0: 1: 1) st, [inc in last st] 0 (0: 0: 0: 1: 1) times. 67 (67: 69: 71: 73: 75) sts.

Row 10 Moss st 18 (18: 19: 20: 21: 22) sts, [K1, P1 tbl] twice, K3, P1 tbl, K1, P1 tbl, K2, P7, K2, P1 tbl, K1, P1 tbl, K3, [P1 tbl, K1] twice, moss st to end.

Row 11 [Inc in first st] 0 (1: 1: 1: 0: 0) times, moss st 18 (17: 18: 19: 21: 22) sts, [P1, K1 tbl] twice, P3, K1 tbl, P1, K1 tbl, P2, C3B, K1, C3F, P2, K1 tbl, P1, K1 tbl, P3, [K1 tbl, P1] twice, moss st to last 0 (1: 1: 1: 0: 0) st, [inc in last st] 0 (1: 1: 1: 0: 0) times. 67 (69: 71: 73: 73: 75) sts.

Row 12 Moss st 18 (19: 20: 21: 21: 22) sts, [K1, P1 tbl] twice, K3, P1 tbl, K1, P1 tbl, K2, P7, K2, P1 tbl, K1, P1 tbl, K3, [P1 tbl, K1] twice, moss st to end.

These 12 rows form patt and start sleeve shaping (for largest 5 sizes).

Cont in patt, shaping sides by inc 1 st at each end of next (11th: 11th: 11th: 9th: 9th) row and every foll

14th (12th: 12th: 12th: 12th: 12th) row until there are 81 (79: 77: 79: 91: 93) sts, taking inc sts into moss st.

97, 102, 107 and 112cm sizes only
Inc 1 st at each end of every foll 16th (14th: 14th: 14th) row until there are 83 (85: 87: 89) sts.

All sizes
Work straight until Sleeve measures 51.5 (51.5: 52.5: 52.5: 52.5: 52.5)cm/20¼ (20¼: 20½: 20½: 20½: 20½)in from cast-on edge, ending with RS facing for next row.

Shape top

Keeping patt correct, cast off 8 (8: 9: 9: 10: 10) sts at beg of next 2 rows. 67 (69: 69: 71: 71: 73) sts.

Dec 1 st at each end of next 5 rows, then on foll 3 alt rows, then on every foll 4th row until 37 (39: 39: 41: 41: 43) sts rem.

Work 1 row.

Dec 1 st at each end of next row and every foll alt row until 29 sts rem, then on foll 3 rows, ending with RS facing for next row.

Cast off rem 23 sts.

HOOD

Using 4mm (US size 6) needles, cast on 85 (85: 85: 89: 89: 89) sts.

Work in moss st as given for Back for 2 rows, ending with RS facing for next row.

Place marker on centre st of last row.

Row 3 (RS) Moss st to marked st, M1, moss st marked st, M1, moss st to end.

Working all increases as set by last row, inc 1 st either side of marked centre back st on 4th row and every foll 4th row until there are 97 (97: 97: 101: 101: 101) sts, taking inc sts into moss st.

Work straight until Hood measures 37cm/14½in from cast-on edge, ending with RS facing for next row.

Next row (RS) Moss st to within 2 sts of marked st, work 2 tog tbl, moss st marked st, work 2 tog, moss st to end.

Working all decreases as set by last row, dec 1 st either side of marked centre back st on 4th row and every foll alt row until 87 (87: 87: 91: 91: 91) sts rem, ending with WS facing for next row.

Next row (WS) Moss st to within 1 st of marked st, work 2 tog (marked st is 2nd of these 2 sts), moss st to end. 86 (86: 86: 90: 90: 90) sts.

Next row Moss st 43 (43: 43: 45: 45: 45) sts and turn.

Fold Hood in half with RS facing each other and, using a spare needle, cast off both sets of 43 (43: 43: 45: 45: 45) sts together by taking one st from one needle with correspond st from other needle (to form top seam of Hood).

MAKING UP

Do NOT press.

Sew shoulder seams. Sew sleeves into armholes. Sew side and sleeve seams, leaving side seams open for first 46 rows.

Hood border

With RS facing and using 3¼mm (US size 3) circular needle, pick up and knit 153 sts evenly along straight row-end edge of Hood.

Row 1 (WS) K3, *P3, K3; rep from * to end.

Row 2 P3, *K3, P3; rep from * to end.

These 2 rows form rib.

Work in rib for 6 rows more, ending with WS facing for next row.

Cast off in rib (on WS).

Matching cast-off edge of Hood Border to front opening edges and easing in Hood to fit, sew cast-on edge of Hood to neck edge.

Pocket tops (both alike)

Slip 37 sts left on pocket holder onto 3¼mm (US size 3) needles and rejoin yarn with RS facing.

Row 1 (RS) P2, K3, *P3, K3; rep from * to last 2 sts, P2.

Row 2 K2, P3, *K3, P3; rep from * to last 2 sts, K2.

These 2 rows form rib.

Work in rib for 6 rows more, ending with WS facing for next row.

Cast off in rib (on WS).

Sew Pocket Linings in place on inside, then neatly sew down ends of Pocket Tops.

Make 4 twisted cords, each 28cm/11in long, and knot one end, leaving a little tassel of approximately 2cm/³⁄₄in. Attach other ends of twisted cords to front opening edges – position top pair of cords just below neck seam, and second pair of cords approximately 8cm/3¼in up from base of front opening.

Hot machine wash completed garment and tumble dry (to shrink to correct length).

92: 95: 97) sts.

Row 1 (RS) K1 (1: 0: 0: 1: 1), *P1, K1; rep from * to end.

Row 2 *K1, P1; rep from * to last 1 (1: 0: 0: 1: 1) st, K1 (1: 0: 0: 1: 1).

These 2 rows form moss st.

Work in moss st until Right Front matches Back to start of armhole shaping, ending with WS facing for next row.

Shape armhole

Keeping moss st correct, cast off 3 sts at beg of next row. 82 (84: 87: 89: 92: 94) sts.

Dec 1 st at armhole edge of next row and 2 foll 4th rows. 79 (81: 84: 86: 89: 91) sts.

Work straight until Right Front matches Back to start of shoulder shaping, ending with WS facing for next row.

Shape shoulder

Cast off 10 (11: 12: 12: 13: 14) sts at beg of next row and foll alt row, then 11 (11: 12: 13: 14: 14) sts at beg of foll alt row, ending with RS facing for next row.

Leave rem 48 (48: 48: 49: 49: 49) sts on a holder and do NOT break off yarn but set aside this ball of yarn to use for Collar.

SLEEVES (make 2)

Using 4mm (US size 6) needles, cast on 55 (55: 57: 59: 59: 61) sts.

Work in moss st as given for Back for 5cm/2in, ending with RS facing for next row.

Inc 1 st at each end of next row and every foll 6th (4th: 6th: 4th: 4th: 4th) row to 89 (65: 95: 65: 65: 73) sts, then on every foll 8th (6th: 8th: 6th: 6th: 6th) row until there are 93 (97: 97: 101: 101: 105) sts, taking inc sts into moss st.

Work straight until Sleeve measures 45 (45: 46: 46: 46: 46)cm/17¾ (17¾: 18: 18: 18: 18)in from cast-on edge, ending with RS facing for next row.

Shape top

Keeping moss st correct, cast off 3 sts at beg of next

6 rows, then 6 sts at beg of foll 8 rows.
Cast off rem 27 (31: 31: 35: 35: 39) sts.

MAKING UP

Press lightly on WS following instructions on yarn label.
Sew shoulder seams.

Collar

With RS facing, using 4mm (US size 6) needles and ball
of yarn set aside with Right Front, moss st across 48 (48:
48: 49: 49: 49) sts on right front holder, pick up and knit
47 (47: 47: 49: 49: 49) sts from back, then moss st across
48 (48: 48: 49: 49: 49) sts on left front holder. 143 (143:
143: 147: 147: 147) sts.
Work in moss st as set by Front sts until Collar measures
5cm/2in from pick-up row, ending with RS facing for
next row.
Cast off in moss st.
Sew sleeves into armholes. Sew side and sleeve seams.
Fasten fronts with a decorative pin if desired.

MOSS STITCH JACKET

Next row (RS) K2, K2tog, K to last 4 sts, K2tog tbl, K2. Working all raglan decreases as set by last row, dec 1 st at each end of 4th row and 7 (6: 7: 7: 6: 7) foll 4th rows, then on every foll alt row until 21 sts rem, ending with RS facing for next row.

Shape neck

Cast off 4 sts at beg and dec 1 st at end of next row. 16 sts.

Work 1 row.

Rep last 2 rows twice more. 6 sts.

Cast off 4 sts at beg of next row. 2 sts.

Work 1 row.

Next row (RS) K2tog and fasten off.

MAKING UP

Press lightly on WS following instructions on yarn label. Sew raglan seams.

Button band

Using 2¾mm (US size 2) needles, cast on 7 sts.

Work in moss st as given for Back until Button Band, when slightly stretched, fits up left front opening edge, from base of front opening to start of neck shaping, sewing in place as you go along and ending with RS facing for next row.

Break off yarn and leave sts on a holder.

Mark positions for 3 buttons on this Band – first to come 1.5cm/⅝in up from base of opening, last to come level with first dec along front opening edge, and rem button spaced evenly between.

Buttonhole band

Using 2¾mm (US size 2) needles, cast on 7 sts.

Work in moss st as given for Back until Buttonhole Band, when slightly stretched, fits up right front opening edge, from base of front opening to start of neck shaping, sewing in place as you go along, ending with RS facing for next row and with the addition of 3 buttonholes worked to correspond with positions marked for buttons on Button Band as follows:

Buttonhole row (RS) Moss st 3 sts, [yfwd] twice (to make a buttonhole, drop extra loop on next row), work 2 tog, moss st 2 sts.

When Band is complete, do NOT break off yarn.

Collar

With RS facing and using 2¾mm (US size 2) needles, moss st 7 sts of Buttonhole Band, pick up and knit

17 (17: 17: 18: 18: 18) sts up right side of neck, 16 sts from top of Right Sleeve, 37 (37: 37: 39: 39: 39) sts from Back, 16 sts from top of Left Sleeve, and 17 (17: 17: 18: 18: 18) sts down left side of neck, then moss st across 7 sts left on Button Band holder. 117 (117: 117: 121: 121: 121) sts.

Keeping moss st correct as set by Band sts, work in moss st for 3 rows, ending with RS of Body (WS of Collar) facing for next row.

Next row Moss st 2 sts, M2, moss st to last 2 sts, M2, moss st 2 sts.

Work 3 rows.

Rep last 4 rows 6 times more. 145 (145: 145: 149: 149: 149) sts.

Cast off in moss st.

Sew side and sleeve seams. Lay Buttonhole Band over Button Band and sew cast-on edges of Bands to cast-off edge at base of front opening. Sew buttons to neck opening and cuffs.

bow sweater

WENDY BAKER

TO FIT BUST

97	102	107	112	117	122	cm
38	40	42	44	46	48	in

FINISHED MEASUREMENTS

Around bust

106	111	116	121	126	131	cm
41¾	43¾	45½	47½	49½	51½	in

Length to back neck

61	61	62	62	63	63	cm
24	24	24½	24½	24¾	24¾	in

Sleeve seam

35	35	36	36	36	36	cm
13¾	13¾	14	14	14	14	in

YARN

8 (9: 9: 10: 10: 10) x 50g/1¾oz balls of Rowan Classic *Cashsoft 4-Ply* in Loganberry 430

NEEDLES

Pair of 3mm (UK no 11) (US size 2) knitting needles
Pair of 3¼mm (UK no 10) (US size 3) knitting needles

TENSION

28 sts and 36 rows to 10cm/4in measured over st st using 3¼mm (US size 3) needles *or size to obtain correct tension.*

ABBREVIATIONS

See page 132.

BACK

Using 3mm (US size 2) needles, cast on 149 (155: 163: 169: 177: 183) sts.

Row 1 (RS) K1, *P1, K1; rep from * to end.

Row 2 As row 1.

These 2 rows form moss st.

Work in moss st for 16 rows more, ending with RS facing for next row.

Change to 3¼mm (US size 3) needles.**

Starting with a K row, work in st st until Back measures 20cm/7¾in from cast-on edge, ending with RS facing for next row.

Change to 3mm (US size 2) needles.

Work straight until Back measures 26cm/10¼in from cast-on edge, ending with RS facing for next row.

Change to 3¼mm (US size 3) needles.

Work straight until Back measures 40cm/15¾in from cast-on edge, ending with RS facing for next row.

Shape raglan armholes

Cast off 7 sts at beg of next 2 rows. 135 (141: 149: 155: 163: 169) sts.

Next row (RS) K2, sl 1, K1, psso, K to last 4 sts, K2tog, K2.

Next row [P2, P2tog] 0 (0: 0: 0: 0: 1) times, P to last 0 (0: 0: 0: 0: 4) sts, [P2tog tbl, P2] 0 (0: 0: 0: 0: 1) times.

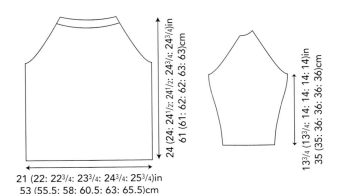

21 (22: 22¾: 23¾: 24¾: 25¾)in
53 (55.5: 58: 60.5: 63: 65.5)cm

24 (24: 24½: 24½: 24¾: 24¾)in
61 (61: 62: 62: 63: 63)cm

13¾ (13¾: 14: 14: 14: 14)in
35 (35: 36: 36: 36: 36)cm

Working all raglan armhole decreases as set by last 2 rows, cont as follows:

Work 2 (2: 2: 2: 0: 0) rows.

Dec 1 st at each end of next 1 (1: 1: 1: 1: 3) rows, then on 8 (6: 3: 2: 0: 0) foll 4th rows, then on every foll alt row until 107 (107: 107: 109: 109: 109) sts rem.

Work 1 row, ending with RS facing for next row.

Shape back neck

Next row (RS) K2, sl 1, K1, psso, K14, K2tog, K2 and turn, leaving rem sts on a holder. 20 sts.

Work each side of neck separately.

Working all neck decreases in same way as raglan armhole decreases, dec 1 st at each end of 2nd row and foll 5 alt rows. 8 sts.

Dec 1 st at raglan armhole edge only on 2nd row and foll 4 alt rows. 3 sts.

Next row (WS) P3.

Next row K1, sl 1, K1, psso.

Next row P2.

Next row K2tog and fasten off.

With RS facing, rejoin yarn to rem sts, cast off centre 63 (63: 63: 65: 65: 65) sts, K2, sl 1, K1, psso, K to last 4 sts, K2tog, K2. 20 sts.

Working all neck decreases in same way as raglan armhole decreases, dec 1 st at each end of 2nd row and foll 5 alt rows. 8 sts.

Dec 1 st at raglan armhole edge only on 2nd row and foll 4 alt rows. 3 sts.

Next row (WS) P3.

Next row K2tog, K1.

Next row P2.

Next row K2tog and fasten off.

FRONT

Work as given for Back to **.

Next row (RS) K39 (41: 44: 46: 49: 51), yfwd, K1, sl 1, K2tog, psso, K1, yfwd, K61 (63: 65: 67: 69: 71), yfwd, K1, sl 1, K2tog, psso, K1, yfwd, K to end.

Next row Purl.

Rep last 2 rows until Front measures 20cm/7¾in from cast-on edge, ending with RS facing for next row.

Change to 3mm (US size 2) needles.

Starting with a K row, work in st st until Front measures 26cm/10¼in from cast-on edge, ending with RS facing for next row.

Change to 3¼mm (US size 3) needles.

Work straight until Front matches Back to start of raglan armhole shaping, ending with RS facing for next row.

Shape raglan armholes

Cast off 7 sts at beg of next 2 rows. 135 (141: 149: 155: 163: 169) sts.

Working all raglan armhole decreases as set by Back, dec 1 st at each end of next 1 (1: 1: 1: 1: 5) rows, then on 5 (6: 4: 3: 0: 0) foll 4th rows, then on foll 0 (0: 5: 8: 15: 14) alt rows. 123 (127: 129: 131: 131: 131) sts.

Work 3 (1: 1: 1: 1: 1) rows, ending with RS facing for next row.

Shape front neck

Next row (RS) [K2, sl 1, K1, psso] 1 (0: 1: 1: 1: 1) times, K33 (39: 36: 36: 36: 36), K2tog, K2 and turn, leaving rem sts on a holder. 39 (42: 42: 42: 42: 42) sts.

Work each side of neck separately.

Working all neck decreases in same way as raglan armhole decreases, dec 1 st at neck edge of 2nd row and foll 17 alt rows **and at the same time** dec 1 st at raglan armhole edge of 4th (2nd: 2nd: 2nd: 2nd: 2nd) row and 2 (0: 0: 0: 0: 0) foll 4th rows, then on foll 12 (17: 17: 17: 17: 17) alt rows. 6 sts.

Next row (WS) P6.

Next row K2, sl 1, K2tog, psso, K1.

Next row P4.

Next row K1, sl 1, K2tog, psso.

Next row P2.

Next row K2tog and fasten off.

With RS facing, rejoin yarn to rem sts, cast off centre 41 (41: 41: 43: 43: 43) sts, K2, sl 1, K1, psso, K to last 4 (0: 4: 4: 4: 4) sts, [K2tog, K2] 1 (0: 1: 1: 1: 1) times. 39 (42: 42: 42: 42: 42) sts.

Working all neck decreases in same way as raglan armhole decreases, dec 1 st at neck edge of 2nd row and foll 17 alt rows **and at the same time** dec 1 st at raglan armhole edge of 4th (2nd: 2nd: 2nd: 2nd: 2nd) row and 2 (0: 0: 0: 0: 0) foll 4th rows, then on foll 12 (17: 17: 17: 17: 17) alt rows. 6 sts.

Next row (WS) P6.

Next row K1, K3tog, K2.

Next row P4.

Next row K3tog, K1.

Next row P2.

Next row K2tog and fasten off.

KNITTING GOES LARGE

SLEEVES (make 2)

Using 3mm (US size 2) needles, cast on 73 (73: 75: 77: 77: 79) sts.

Work in moss st as given for Back for 18 rows, ending with RS facing for next row.

Change to 3¼mm (US size 3) needles.

Next row (RS) K34 (34: 35: 36: 36: 37), yfwd, K1, sl 1, K2tog, psso, K1, yfwd, K to end.

Next row Purl.

These 2 rows form patt.

Next row K4, M1, patt to last 4 sts, M1, K4.

Working all sleeve increases as set by last row, inc 1 st at each end of 4th row and 4 (6: 5: 5: 6: 6) foll 4th rows, then on 1 (0: 0: 0: 0: 0) foll 6th row. 87 (89: 89: 91: 93: 95) sts.

Work in patt for 3 (1: 5: 5: 1: 1) rows more, ending with RS facing for next row.

Starting with a K row, work in st st, inc 1 st at each end of 3rd (3rd: next: next: 3rd: 3rd) row and 0 (0: 0: 0: 1: 1) foll 4th row, then on every foll 6th row until there are 109 (111: 113: 115: 117: 119) sts.

Work straight until Sleeve measures 35 (35: 36: 36: 36: 36)cm/13¾ (13¾: 14: 14: 14: 14)in from cast-on edge, ending with RS facing for next row.

Shape raglan

Cast off 7 sts at beg of next 2 rows. 95 (97: 99: 101: 103: 105) sts.

Working all raglan decreases in same way as for raglan armholes, dec 1 st at each end of next row and every foll alt row until 29 sts rem.

Work 1 row.

Left sleeve only

Dec 1 st at each end of next row, then cast off 6 sts at beg of foll row. 21 sts.

Dec 1 st at beg of next row, then cast off 6 sts at beg of foll row. 14 sts.

Right sleeve only

Cast off 7 sts at beg and dec 1 st at end of next row. 21 sts.

Work 1 row.

Cast off 6 sts at beg and dec 1 st at end of next row. 14 sts.

Work 1 row.

Both sleeves

Rep last 2 rows once more.

Cast off rem 7 sts.

MAKING UP

Press lightly on WS following instructions on yarn label. Sew both front and right back raglan seams.

Neckband

With RS facing and using 3¼mm (US size 3) needles, pick up and knit 21 sts from top of left sleeve, 31 sts down left side of neck, 41 sts from front, 31 sts up right side of neck, 21 sts from top of right sleeve, 16 sts down right side of back neck, 63 sts from back, then 16 sts up left side of back neck. 240 sts.

Row 1 (WS) *K1, P1; rep from * to end.

Row 2 *P1, K1; rep from * to end.

These 2 rows form moss st.

Work in moss st for 5 rows more, ending with RS facing for next row.

Row 8 (RS) *Moss st 7 sts, work 3 tog; rep from * to end. 192 sts.

Change to 3mm (US size 2) needles.

Work in moss st for 5 rows, ending with RS facing for next row.

Row 14 (RS) *Moss st 13 sts, work 3 tog; rep from * to end. 168 sts.

Work in moss st for 3 rows, ending with RS facing for next row.

Cast off in moss st.

Sew left back raglan and Neckband seam. Sew side and sleeve seams.

Bow

Using 3mm (US size 2) needles, cast on 21 sts.

Work in moss st as given for Back, inc 1 st at each end of 2nd row and foll 4 alt rows. 31 sts.

Work 3 rows, ending with WS facing for next row.

Dec 1 st at each end of next row and foll 4 alt rows, ending with RS facing for next row.

Cast off rem 21 sts in moss st.

Bow Centre

Using 3mm (US size 2) needles, cast on 5 sts.

Work in moss st as given for Back for 23 rows, ending with WS facing for next row.

Cast off in moss st (on WS).

Sew together cast-on and cast-off ends of Bow Centre to form a loop. Slip Bow through Bow Centre and attach to Neckband as shown.

split neck tunic

KIM HARGREAVES

TO FIT BUST						
97	102	107	112	117	122	cm
38	40	42	44	46	48	in
FINISHED MEASUREMENTS						
Around bust						
128	133	138	143	149	154	cm
50¼	52¼	54¼	56¼	58½	60½	in
Length to shoulder						
74	75	76	77	78	79	cm
29	29½	30	30¼	30¾	31	in
Sleeve seam						
46	46	47	47	47	47	cm
18	18	18½	18½	18½	18½	in

YARN

16 (17: 18: 19: 19: 20) x 50g/1¾oz balls of Rowan *Cotton Glace* in Sky 749

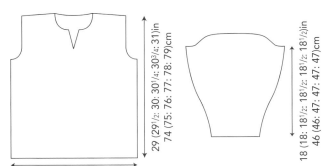

29 (29½: 30: 30¼: 30¾: 31)in
74 (75: 76: 77: 78: 79)cm

18 (18: 18½: 18½: 18½: 18½)in
46 (46: 47: 47: 47: 47)cm

25¼ (26¼: 27¼: 28¼: 29¼: 30¼)in
64 (66.5: 69: 71.5: 74.5: 77)cm

K2tog, K2 and turn, leaving rem sts on a holder.
Work each side of neck separately.
Working all neck decreases in same way as raglan armhole decreases and keeping raglan armhole decreases correct, dec 1 st at raglan armhole edge of 2nd (2nd: 2nd: 2nd: 2nd: next) row and foll 0 (0: 0: 0: 0: 3) rows, then on foll 23 (24: 25: 26: 27: 27) alt rows **and at the same time** dec 1 st at neck edge of 2nd row and every foll alt row. 20 sts.

Dec 1 st at raglan armhole edge only on 2nd row and every foll alt row until 3 sts rem.
Work 1 row, ending with RS facing for next row.
Next row (RS) K1, sl 1, K1, psso.
Next row P2.
Next row K2tog and fasten off.
With RS facing, slip centre 2 sts onto a holder, rejoin yarn to rem sts, K2, sl 1, K1, psso, K to last 4 sts, K2tog, K2.
Complete to match first side, reversing shapings.

SLEEVES (make 2)

Using 3mm (US size 2) needles and MC, cast on 72 (72: 74: 76: 76: 78) sts.

Noting that first row is a WS row, work in garter st for 10cm/4in, ending with RS facing for next row.

Change to 3¾mm (US size 5) needles.

Starting and ending rows as indicated, and joining in and breaking off colours as required, now work in patt from Sleeve Chart (see page 65) as follows:

Inc 1 st at each end of 3rd and 10 foll 4th rows, taking inc sts into patt. 94 (94: 96: 98: 98: 100) sts.

Work 3 rows, ending after chart row 46 and with RS facing for next row.

Break off contrasting colours and cont using MC only.

Change to 3mm (US size 2) needles.

Work in garter st for 6 rows, inc 1 st at each end of next row and foll 0 (4th: 4th: 4th: 4th: 4th) of these rows and ending with RS facing for next row.

96 (98: 100: 102: 102: 104) sts.

Change to 3¼mm (US size 3) needles.

Starting with a K row, work in st st, inc 1 st at each end of next (3rd: 5th: 5th: 3rd: 3rd) row and 0 (1: 0: 0: 2: 2) foll 4th rows, then on every foll 6th row until there are 114 (116: 118: 120: 122: 124) sts.

Work straight until Sleeve measures 43 (43: 44: 44: 44: 44)cm/17 (17: 17¼: 17¼: 17¼: 17¼)in from cast-on edge, ending with RS facing for next row.

Shape raglan

Cast off 7 sts at beg of next 2 rows. 100 (102: 104: 106: 108: 110) sts.

Working all raglan decreases in same way as given for raglan armhole decreases, dec 1 st at each end of next row and 10 foll 4th rows, then on every foll alt row until 22 sts rem.

Work 1 row, ending with RS facing for next row.

Cast off.

MAKING UP

Press lightly on WS following instructions on yarn label.

Sew both front and right back raglan seams.

Neckband

With RS facing, using 3mm (US size 2) circular needle and MC, pick up and knit 20 sts from top of left sleeve, 60 (62: 64: 66: 68: 70) sts down left side of neck, K 2 sts left on holder at base of V and place a marker between these sts, pick up and knit 60 (62: 64: 66: 68: 70) sts up right side of neck, 20 sts from top of right sleeve, 6 sts down right side of back neck, 44 (44: 44: 46: 46: 46) sts from back, then 6 sts up left side of back neck. 218 (222: 226: 232: 236: 240) sts.

Row 1 (WS) Knit.

Row 2 K to within 2 sts of marker, K2tog, slip marker onto right needle, sl 1, K1, psso, K to end.

Rep last 2 rows 3 times more, and then first of these 2 rows again, ending with RS facing for next row. 210 (214: 218: 224: 228: 232) sts.

Cast off knitwise, still decreasing at each side of marker as before.

Sew side, sleeve seams and right front raglan seam.

lacy cardigan

KIM HARGREAVES

<table>
<tr><td colspan="7">TO FIT BUST</td></tr>
<tr><td>97</td><td>102</td><td>107</td><td>112</td><td>117</td><td>122</td><td>cm</td></tr>
<tr><td>38</td><td>40</td><td>42</td><td>44</td><td>46</td><td>48</td><td>in</td></tr>
<tr><td colspan="7">FINISHED MEASUREMENTS</td></tr>
<tr><td colspan="7">Around bust</td></tr>
<tr><td>105</td><td>109</td><td>114</td><td>119</td><td>124</td><td>128</td><td>cm</td></tr>
<tr><td>41¼</td><td>43</td><td>44¾</td><td>46¾</td><td>48¾</td><td>50¼</td><td>in</td></tr>
<tr><td colspan="7">Length to shoulder</td></tr>
<tr><td>58</td><td>59</td><td>60</td><td>61</td><td>62</td><td>63</td><td>cm</td></tr>
<tr><td>22¾</td><td>23¼</td><td>23½</td><td>24</td><td>24½</td><td>24¾</td><td>in</td></tr>
<tr><td colspan="7">Sleeve seam</td></tr>
<tr><td>43</td><td>43</td><td>44</td><td>44</td><td>44</td><td>44</td><td>cm</td></tr>
<tr><td>17</td><td>17</td><td>17¼</td><td>17¼</td><td>17¼</td><td>17¼</td><td>in</td></tr>
</table>

YARN

11 (12: 12: 13: 13: 14) x 50g/1¾oz balls of Rowan *4-Ply Cotton* in Cream 153

NEEDLES

Pair of 3mm (UK no 11) (US size 3) knitting needles
2¼mm (UK no 13) (US size 1) circular knitting needle

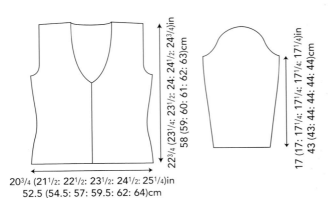

20¾ (21½: 22½: 23½: 24½: 25¼)in
52.5 (54.5: 57: 59.5: 62: 64)cm

22¾ (23¼: 23½: 24: 24½: 24¾)in
58 (59: 60: 61: 62: 63)cm

17 (17: 17¼: 17¼: 17¼: 17¼)in
43 (43: 44: 44: 44: 44)cm

EXTRAS

7 buttons

TENSION

34 sts and 38 rows to 10cm/4in measured over patt using 3mm (US size 3) needles *or size to obtain correct tension.*

ABBREVIATIONS

See page 132.

BACK

Using 2¼mm (US size 1) circular needle, cast on 533 (557: 581: 605: 629: 653) sts.

Row 1 (RS) K1, *K2, lift first of these 2 sts over 2nd st and off right needle; rep from * to end. 267 (279: 291: 303: 315: 327) sts.

Row 2 *P1, P2tog; rep from * to end. 178 (186: 194: 202: 210: 218) sts.

These 2 rows form frill edging.

Change to 3mm (US size 3) needles.

Now work in patt as follows:

Row 1 (RS) K0 (1: 2: 0: 1: 2), [P1, yon, K2tog tbl] 0 (1: 0: 0: 1: 0) times, P1, *K2, P1, yon, K2tog tbl, P1; rep from * to last 3 (1: 5: 3: 1: 5) sts, K2 (1: 2: 2: 1: 2), P1 (0: 1: 1: 0: 1), K0 (0: 2: 0: 0: 2).

Row 2 P0 (1: 2: 0: 1: 2), K1, *P2, K1; rep from * to last 0 (1: 2: 0: 1: 2) sts, P0 (1: 2: 0: 1: 2).

Row 3 K0 (1: 2: 0: 1: 2), [P1, K2tog, yfrn] 0 (1: 0: 0: 1: 0) times, P1, *K2, P1, K2tog, yfrn, P1; rep from * to last 3 (1: 5: 3: 1: 5) sts, K2 (1: 2: 2: 1: 2), P1 (0: 1: 1: 0: 1), K0 (0: 2: 0: 0: 2).

Row 4 As row 2.

These 4 rows form patt.

Work in patt for 18 rows more, ending with RS facing for next row.

Keeping patt correct, dec 1 st at each end of next row and every foll 4th row until 162 (170: 178: 186: 194: 202) sts rem.

Work straight until Back measures 18 (18: 19: 19: 20: 20)cm/7 (7: 7½: 7½: 7¾: 7¾)in from cast-on edge, ending with RS facing for next row.

Inc 1 st at each end of next row and every foll 8th row until there are 178 (186: 194: 202: 210: 218) sts, taking inc sts into patt.

Work 19 rows, ending with RS facing for next row.

Shape armholes

Keeping patt correct, cast off 6 (6: 7: 7: 8: 8) sts at beg of next 2 rows, then 3 sts at beg of foll 2 rows. 160 (168: 174: 182: 188: 196) sts.

Dec 1 st at each end of next 7 (9: 9: 11: 11: 13) rows, then on foll 9 (9: 10: 10: 11: 11) alt rows, then on 6 foll 4th rows. 116 (120: 124: 128: 132: 136) sts.

Work straight until armhole measures 20 (21: 21: 22: 22: 23)cm/7¾ (8¼: 8¼: 8½: 8½: 9)in, ending with RS facing for next row.

Shape back neck and shoulders

Cast off 10 (10: 11: 11: 12: 13) sts at beg of next 2 rows. 96 (100: 102: 106: 108: 110) sts.

Next row (RS) Cast off 10 (10: 11: 11: 12: 13) sts, patt until there are 13 (15: 15: 16: 16: 16) sts on right needle and turn, leaving rem sts on a holder.

Work each side of neck separately.

Cast off 4 sts at beg of next row.

Cast off rem 9 (11: 11: 12: 12: 12) sts.

With RS facing, rejoin yarn to rem sts, cast off centre 50 (50: 50: 52: 52: 52) sts, patt to end.

Complete to match first side, reversing shapings.

LEFT FRONT

Using 2¼mm (US size 1) circular needle, cast on 263 (275: 287: 299: 311: 323) sts.

Work frill edging rows 1 and 2 as given for Back. 88 (92: 96: 100: 104: 108) sts.

Change to 3mm (US size 3) needles.

Now work in patt as follows:

Row 1 (RS) K0 (1: 2: 0: 1: 2), [P1, yon, K2tog tbl] 0 (1: 0: 0: 1: 0) times, P1, *K2, P1, yon, K2tog tbl, P1; rep from *

to last 3 sts, K2, P1.

Row 2 K1, *P2, K1; rep from * to last 0 (1: 2: 0: 1: 2) sts, P0 (1: 2: 0: 1: 2).

Row 3 K0 (1: 2: 0: 1: 2), [P1, K2tog, yfrn] 0 (1: 0: 0: 1: 0) times, P1, *K2, P1, K2tog, yfrn, P1; rep from * to last 3 sts, K2, P1.

Row 4 As row 2.

These 4 rows form patt.

Work in patt for 18 rows more, ending with RS facing for next row.

Keeping patt correct, dec 1 st at beg of next row and every foll 4th row until 80 (84: 88: 92: 96: 100) sts rem. Work straight until Left Front measures 18 (18: 19: 19: 20: 20)cm/7 (7: 7½: 7½: 7¾: 7¾)in from cast-on edge, ending with RS facing for next row.

Inc 1 st at beg of next row and every foll 8th row until there are 88 (92: 96: 100: 104: 108) sts, taking inc sts into patt.

Work 5 rows, ending with RS facing for next row.

Shape front slope

Keeping patt correct, dec 1 st at end of next row and foll 5 alt rows. 82 (86: 90: 94: 98: 102) sts.

Work 1 row, ending with RS facing for next row.

Shape armhole

Keeping patt correct, cast off 6 (6: 7: 7: 8: 8) sts at beg of next row, then 3 sts at beg of foll alt row **and at the same time** dec 1 st at front slope edge of next row and foll alt row. 71 (75: 78: 82: 85: 89) sts.

Work 1 row.

Dec 1 st at armhole edge of next 7 (9: 9: 11: 11: 13) rows, then on foll 9 (9: 10: 10: 11: 11) alt rows, then on 6 foll 4th rows **and at the same time** dec 1 st at front slope edge of next row and foll 8 (6: 6: 6: 6: 4) alt rows, then on every foll 4th row. 32 (35: 36: 38: 39: 42) sts.

Dec 1 st at front slope edge only on 4th (2nd: 4th: 2nd: 4th: 2nd) row and every foll 4th row until 29 (31: 33: 34: 36: 38) sts rem.

Work straight until Left Front matches Back to start of shoulder shaping, ending with RS facing for next row.

Shape shoulder

Cast off 10 (10: 11: 11: 12: 13) sts at beg of next row and foll alt row.

Work 1 row.

Cast off rem 9 (11: 11: 12: 12: 12) sts.

KNITTING GOES LARGE

RIGHT FRONT

Using 2¼mm (US size 1) circular needle, cast on 263 (275: 287: 299: 311: 323) sts.

Work frill edging rows 1 and 2 as given for Back. 88 (92: 96: 100: 104: 108) sts.

Change to 3mm (US size 3) needles.

Now work in patt as follows:

Row 1 (RS) P1, *K2, P1, yon, K2tog tbl, P1; rep from * to last 3 (1: 5: 3: 1: 5) sts, K2 (1: 2: 2: 1: 2), P1 (0: 1: 1: 0: 1), K0 (0: 2: 0: 0: 2).

Row 2 P0 (1: 2: 0: 1: 2), K1, *P2, K1; rep from * to end.

Row 3 P1, *K2, P1, K2tog, yfrn, P1; rep from * to last 3 (1: 5: 3: 1: 5) sts, K2 (1: 2: 2: 1: 2), P1 (0: 1: 1: 0: 1), K0 (0: 2: 0: 0: 2).

Row 4 As row 2.

These 4 rows form patt.

Work in patt for 18 rows more, ending with RS facing for next row.

Keeping patt correct, dec 1 st at end of next row and every foll 4th row until 80 (84: 88: 92: 96: 100) sts rem.

Complete to match Left Front, reversing shapings.

SLEEVES (make 2)

Using 2¼mm (US size 1) circular needle, cast on 257 (257: 263: 269: 269: 275) sts.

Work frill edging rows 1 and 2 as given for Back. 86 (86: 88: 90: 90: 92) sts.

Change to 3mm (US size 3) needles.

Now work in patt as follows:

Row 1 (RS) K2 (2: 0: 1: 1: 2), [P1, yon, K2tog tbl] 0 (0: 1: 1: 1: 1) times, P1, *K2, P1, yon, K2tog tbl, P1; rep from * to last 5 (5: 0: 1: 1: 2) sts, K2 (2: 0: 1: 1: 2), [P1, K2] 1 (1: 0: 0: 0: 0) times.

Row 2 P2 (2: 0: 1: 1: 2), K1, *P2, K1; rep from * to last 2 (2: 0: 1: 1: 2) sts, P2 (2: 0: 1: 1: 2).

Row 3 K2 (2: 0: 1: 1: 2), [P1, K2tog, yfrn] 0 (0: 1: 1: 1: 1) times, P1, *K2, P1, K2tog, yfrn, P1; rep from * to last 5 (5: 0: 1: 1: 2) sts, K2 (2: 0: 1: 1: 2), [P1, K2] 1 (1: 0: 0: 0: 0) times.

Row 4 As row 2.

These 4 rows form patt.

Work in patt, shaping sides by inc 1 st at each end of 3rd (3rd: 3rd: 3rd: next: next) row and every foll 8th (8th: 8th: 8th: 6th: 6th) row until there are 112 (122: 120: 122: 94: 96) sts, taking inc sts into patt.

97, 107, 112, 117 and 122cm sizes only

Inc 1 st at each end of every foll 10th (10th: 10th: 8th: 8th) row until there are 120 (124: 126: 128: 130) sts.

All sizes

Work straight until Sleeve measures 43 (43: 44: 44: 44: 44)cm/17 (17: 17¼: 17¼: 17¼: 17¼)in from cast-on edge, ending with RS facing for next row.

Shape top

Keeping patt correct, cast off 6 (6: 7: 7: 8: 8) sts at beg of next 2 rows. 108 (110: 110: 112: 112: 114) sts.

Dec 1 st at each end of next 5 rows, then on foll 5 alt rows, then on every foll 4th row until 74 (76: 76: 78: 78: 80) sts rem.

Work 1 row.

Dec 1 st at each end of next row and every foll alt row until 62 sts rem, then on foll 7 rows, ending with RS facing for next row. 48 sts.

Cast off 8 sts at beg of next 2 rows.

Cast off rem 32 sts.

MAKING UP

Press lightly on WS following instructions on yarn label. Sew shoulder seams.

Front band

With RS facing and using 2¼mm (US size 1) circular needles, starting and ending at cast-on edges, pick up and knit 102 (102: 105: 105: 108: 108) sts up right front opening edge to start of front slope shaping, place marker on right needle, 78 (81: 81: 85: 85: 88) sts up right front slope to shoulder, 58 (58: 58: 60: 60: 60) sts from back, 78 (81: 81: 85: 85: 88) sts down left front slope to start of front slope shaping, then 102 (102: 105: 105: 108: 108) sts down left front opening edge. 418 (424: 430: 440: 446: 452) sts.

Row 1 (WS) K to marker, slip marker onto right needle, K2 (2: 0: 0: 2: 2), *K2tog, yfwd (to make a buttonhole), K14 (14: 15: 15: 15: 15); rep from * 5 times more, K2tog, yfwd (to make 7th buttonhole), K2 (2: 1: 1: 2: 2).

Row 2 Knit.

Cast off knitwise (on WS).

Sew sleeves into armholes. Sew side and sleeve seams. Sew on buttons.

Now work in patt as follows:

Row 1 (RS) K3 (7: 3: 7: 3: 7), P1, *K7, P1; rep from * to last 3 (7: 3: 7: 3: 7) sts, K3 (7: 3: 7: 3: 7).

Row 2 Purl.

These 2 rows form patt.

Counting in from both ends of last row, place markers on 40th (44th: 48th: 44th: 48th: 52nd) st in from both ends of row – there should be 71 (71: 71: 87: 87: 87) sts at centre of row between marked sts.

Row 3 (RS) K2tog, [patt to within 2 sts of marked st, sl 1, K1, psso, K marked st, K2tog] twice, patt to last 2 sts, K2tog.

Work 15 rows.

Rep last 16 rows twice more, then row 3 again. 127 (135: 143: 151: 159: 167) sts.

Work 19 rows, ending with RS facing for next row.

Next row (RS) Inc in first st, [patt to marked st, M1, K marked st, M1] twice, patt to last st, inc in last st.

Work 13 rows.

Rep last 14 rows twice more, then first of these rows again. 151 (159: 167: 175: 183: 191) sts.

Work straight in patt until Back measures 41 (41: 42: 42: 43: 43)cm/16 (16: 16½: 16½: 17: 17)in from cast-on edge, ending with RS facing for next row.

Shape armholes

Keeping patt correct, cast off 11 (12: 12: 13: 13: 14) sts at beg of next 2 rows. 129 (135: 143: 149: 157: 163) sts.

Dec 1 st at each end of next 11 (13: 13: 15: 15: 17) rows, then on foll 6 (6: 8: 8: 10: 10) alt rows, then on 4 foll 4th rows. 87 (89: 93: 95: 99: 101) sts.

Work straight until armhole measures 21 (22: 22: 23: 23: 24)cm/8¼ (8½: 8½: 9: 9: 9½)in, ending with RS facing for next row.

Shape back neck and shoulders

Cast off 6 (7: 7: 7: 8: 8) sts at beg of next 2 rows. 75 (75: 79: 81: 83: 85) sts.

Next row (RS) Cast off 6 (7: 7: 7: 8: 8) sts, patt until there are 11 (10: 12: 12: 12: 13) sts on right needle and turn, leaving rem sts on a holder.

Work each side of neck separately.

Cast off 4 sts at beg of next row.

Cast off rem 7 (6: 8: 8: 8: 9) sts.

With RS facing, rejoin yarn to rem sts, cast off centre 41 (41: 41: 43: 43: 43) sts, patt to end.

Complete to match first side, reversing shapings.

LEFT FRONT

Centre lower panel

Using 2¼mm (US size 1) needles, cast on 37 (37: 37: 45: 45: 45) sts.

Work in moss st as given for Lower Centre Panel of Back for 6 rows.

Row 7 (RS) Moss st 2 sts, M2, moss st to end.

Work 5 rows.

Row 13 As row 7. 41 (41: 41: 49: 49: 49) sts.

Work 3 rows, ending with RS facing for next row.

Break off yarn and leave sts on a holder.

Left lower panel

Work as given for Right Lower Panel of Back.

Join panels

Row 17 (RS) Moss st first 39 (43: 47: 43: 47: 51) sts of Left Lower Panel, with WS of Centre Lower Panel against RS of Left Lower Panel K tog first st of Centre Lower Panel and last st of Left Lower Panel, moss st next 35 (35: 35: 43: 43: 43) sts of Centre Lower Panel and turn, leaving rem 5 sts on a holder. 75 (79: 83: 87: 91: 95) sts.

Row 18 Purl.

Change to 3mm (US size 3) needles.

Now work in patt as follows:

Row 1 (RS) K3 (7: 3: 7: 3: 7), *P1, K7; rep from * to end.

Row 2 Purl.

These 2 rows form patt.

Counting in from end of last row, place marker on 40th (44th: 48th: 44th: 48th: 52nd) st in from end of row – there should be 35 (35: 35: 43: 43: 43) sts beyond marked st.

Row 3 (RS) K2tog, patt to within 2 sts of marked st, sl 1, K1, psso, K marked st, K2tog, patt to end.

Work 15 rows.

Rep last 16 rows twice more, then row 3 again. 63 (67: 71: 75: 79: 83) sts.

Work 19 rows, ending with RS facing for next row.

Next row (RS) Inc in first st, patt to marked st, M1, K marked st, M1, patt to end.

Work 13 rows.

Rep last 14 rows twice more, then first of these rows again. 75 (79: 83: 87: 91: 95) sts.

Work straight in patt until Left Front matches Back to start of armhole shaping, ending with RS facing for next row.

Shape armhole

Keeping patt correct, cast off 11 (12: 12: 13: 13: 14) sts

at beg of next row. 64 (67: 71: 74: 78: 81) sts.

Work 1 row.

Dec 1 st at armhole edge of next 11 (13: 13: 15: 15: 17) rows, then on foll 6 (6: 8: 8: 10: 10) alt rows, then on 1 (2: 1: 1: 0: 1) foll 4th rows. 46 (46: 49: 50: 53: 53) sts.

Work 2 (0: 0: 2: 2: 0) rows, ending with WS facing for next row.

Shape neck

Keeping patt correct, cast off 9 sts at beg of next row, then 4 sts at beg of foll alt row **and at the same time** dec 1 (0: 0: 1: 1: 0) st at armhole edge of 2nd of these rows. 32 (33: 36: 36: 39: 40) sts.

Dec 1 st at neck edge of next 5 rows, then on foll 3 (3: 3: 4: 4: 4) alt rows, then on 3 foll 4th rows **and at the same time** dec 1 st at armhole edge of 3rd (next: next: 3rd: 3rd: next) and 0 (1: 2: 1: 2: 2) foll 4th rows. 20 (20: 22: 22: 24: 25) sts.

Work straight until Left Front matches Back to start of shoulder shaping, ending with RS facing for next row.

Shape shoulder

Cast off 6 (7: 7: 7: 8: 8) sts at beg of next row and foll alt row.

Work 1 row.

Cast off rem 8 (6: 8: 8: 8: 9) sts.

RIGHT FRONT

Right lower panel

Work as given for Left Lower Panel of Back.

Break off yarn and leave sts on a holder.

Centre lower panel

Using 2¼mm (US size 1) needles, cast on 37 (37: 37: 45: 45: 45) sts.

Work in moss st as given for Lower Centre Panel of Back for 4 rows.

Row 5 (buttonhole row) (RS) Moss st 1 st, work 2 tog, [yrn] twice (to make a buttonhole, drop extra loop on next row), moss st to end.

Work 1 row.

Row 7 (RS) Moss st to last 2 sts, M2, moss st 2 sts.

Work 5 rows.

Row 13 As row 7. 41 (41: 41: 49: 49: 49) sts.

Work 3 rows, ending with RS facing for next row.

Join panels

Row 17 (RS) Moss st first 5 sts of Centre Lower Panel and slip these 5 sts onto a holder, moss st next 35 (35:

35: 43: 43: 43) sts of Centre Lower Panel, with WS of Centre Lower Panel against RS of Right Lower Panel, K tog last st of Centre Lower Panel and first st of Right Lower Panel, moss st rem 39 (43: 47: 43: 47: 51) sts of Right Lower Panel. 75 (79: 83: 87: 91: 95) sts.

Row 18 Purl.

Change to 3mm (US size 3) needles.

Now work in patt as follows:

Row 1 (RS) *K7, P1; rep from * to last 3 (7: 3: 7: 3: 7) sts, K3 (7: 3: 7: 3: 7).

Row 2 Purl.

These 2 rows form patt.

Counting in from beg of last row, place marker on 40th (44th: 48th: 44th: 48th: 52nd) st in from end of row – there should be 35 (35: 35: 43: 43: 43) sts beyond marked st.

Row 3 (RS) Patt to within 2 sts of marked st, sl 1, K1, psso, K marked st, K2tog, patt to last 2 sts, K2tog.

Complete to match Left Front, reversing shapings.

MAKING UP

Press lightly on WS following instructions on yarn label.

Sew shoulder seams.

Button band

Slip 5 sts on left front holder onto 2¼mm (US size 1) needles and rejoin yarn with RS facing.

Work in moss st as set until Button Band, when slightly stretched, fits up left front opening edge to neck shaping, ending with RS facing for next row.

Break off yarn and leave sts on a holder.

Slip stitch band in place. Mark positions for 7 buttons on this band – first to come level with buttonhole already made in Right Front, last to come just above neck shaping, and rem 5 buttons evenly spaced between.

Buttonhole band

Slip 5 sts on right front holder onto 2¼mm (US size 1) needles and rejoin yarn with WS facing.

Work in moss st as set until Buttonhole Band, when slightly stretched, fits up right front opening edge to neck shaping, ending with RS facing for next row and with the addition of 5 more buttonholes worked to correspond with positions marked for buttons on Left Front as follows:

Buttonhole row (RS) Moss st 1 st, work 2 tog, [yrn] twice (to make a buttonhole, drop extra loop on next row), moss st 2 sts.

When band is complete, do NOT break off yarn.
Slip stitch band in place.

Neckband

With RS facing and using 2¼mm (US size 1) needles,
moss st across 5 sts of Buttonhole Band, pick up and
knit 63 (63: 63: 64: 64: 64) sts up right side of neck,
49 (49: 49: 51: 51: 51) sts from back, and 63 (63: 63: 64:
64: 64) sts down left side of neck, then moss st across
5 sts of Button Band. 185 (185: 185: 189: 189: 189) sts.
Keeping sts correct as set by bands, work in moss st
across all sts as follows:
Work 1 row, ending with RS facing for next row.
Row 2 (RS) Moss st 1 st, work 2 tog, [yrn] twice (to make
7th buttonhole, drop extra loop on next row), moss st
to end.
Work in moss st for 3 rows more, ending with RS facing
for next row.
Cast off in moss st.

Armhole borders (both alike)

With RS facing and using 2¼mm (US size 1) needles,
pick up and knit 143 (151: 151: 159: 159: 167) sts evenly
all around armhole edge.
Work in moss st as given for Lower Centre Panel of Back
for 5 rows, ending with RS facing for next row.
Cast off in moss st.
Sew side and Armhole Border seams. Sew on buttons.

scarf and stole

JENNIE ATKINSON

SIZES

Scarf

The finished scarf measures 38cm/15in by 130cm/51in, excluding fringe.

Stole

The finished stole measures 60cm/23½in by 157cm/62in, excluding fringe.

(**Note:** The Scarf is shown on the opposite page and the Stole on pages 106 and 107.)

YARNS

Scarf

3 x 25g/⅞oz balls of Rowan *Kidsilk Haze* in Blushes 583

Stole

5 x 25g/⅞oz balls of Rowan *Kidsilk Haze* in Hurricane 632

NEEDLES

Pair of 4mm (UK no 8) (US size 6) knitting needles

EXTRAS

Scarf

Approximately 1,310 small silvered glass beads

Stole

Approximately 1,566 small silvered glass beads

TENSION

24 sts and 32 rows to 10cm/4in measured over st st using 4mm (US size 6) needles *or size to obtain correct tension.*

ABBREVIATIONS

See page 132.

SPECIAL ABBREVIATION

bead 1 = place a bead by bringing yarn to front (RS) of work and slipping bead up next to stitch just worked, slip next stitch purlwise from left needle to right needle and take yarn back to back (WS) of work, leaving bead sitting in front of slipped stitch on RS of knitting.

BEADING NOTE

Before starting to knit, thread the beads onto the knitting yarn. To do this, thread a fine sewing needle (one that will easily pass through the beads) with a short length of sewing thread. Knot the ends of the thread together and then pass the end of the yarn through this loop. Thread a bead onto the sewing thread and then gently slide it along and onto the knitting yarn. Continue in this way until the required number of beads are on the yarn.

scarf

Thread half the beads onto yarn.

Using 4mm (US size 6) needles, cast on 91 sts very loosely.

Row 1 (RS) Knit.

Row 2 and every foll alt row K3, P85, K3.

Row 3 K4, [K5, bead 1, K6] 7 times, K3.

Row 5 K4, [K4, bead 1, K1, bead 1, K5] 7 times, K3.

Row 7 K4, *[K3, bead 1] twice, K4; rep from * to last 3 sts, K3.

Row 9 K4, *[K2, bead 1] 3 times, K3; rep from * to last 3 sts, K3.

Row 11 K4, *[K1, bead 1, K2, bead 1] twice, K2; rep from * to last 3 sts, K3.

Row 13 K4, *bead 1, K2, [bead 1, K1] twice, bead 1, K2, bead 1, K1; rep from * to last 3 sts, K3.

Row 15 K3, bead 1, *K2, [bead 1, K1] 3 times, bead 1, K2, bead 1; rep from * to last 3 sts, K3.

Row 17 K4, *[K1, bead 1] 5 times, K2; rep from * to last 3 sts, K3.

Row 19 As row 15.

Row 21 As row 13.

Row 23 As row 11.

Row 25 As row 9.

Row 27 As row 7.

Row 29 As row 5.

Row 30 As row 2.

Rows 31–58 As rows 3–30.

Rows 59 and 60 As rows 3 and 4.

These 60 rows complete beaded border.

Break off yarn and remove beads.

Rejoin yarn and work lace section as follows:

Row 61 (RS) K4, *yfwd, sl 1, K1, psso, K1, K2tog, yfwd, K1; rep from * to last 3 sts, K3.

Row 62 and every foll alt row K3, P85, K3.

Row 63 K4, *yfwd, K1, sl 1, K2tog, psso, K1, yfwd, K1; rep from * to last 3 sts, K3.

Row 65 K4, *K2tog, yfwd, K1, yfwd, sl 1, K1, psso, K1; rep from * to last 3 sts, K3.

Row 67 K3, K2tog, *[K1, yfwd] twice, K1, sl 1, K2tog, psso; rep from * to last 8 sts, [K1, yfwd] twice, K1, sl 1, K1, psso, K3.

Row 69 K3, *K4, K2tog, yfwd, K1, yfwd, sl 1, K1, psso, K3; rep from * to last 4 sts, K4.

Row 70 As row 62.

Rep last 2 rows until Scarf measures 109cm/43in, ending with RS facing for next row.

Next row As row 65.

Next row As row 62.

Next row As row 67.

Next row As row 62.

Next row As row 61.

Next row As row 62.

Next row As row 63.

Next row As row 62.

Break off yarn and thread on rem beads.

Rejoin yarn and work second beaded border by repeating rows 3–60.

Cast off very loosely.

MAKING UP

Press lightly on WS following instructions on yarn label and taking care not to damage beads.

Cut 300 lengths of yarn, each 38cm/15in long, and knot groups of 10 of these lengths through cast-on and cast-off edges to form fringe, positioning 15 knots evenly spaced along each end.

stole

Thread half the beads onto yarn.

Using 4mm (US size 6) needles, cast on 143 sts very loosely.

(**Note:** Stole is shown on pages 106 and 107.)

Row 1 (RS) Knit.

Row 2 and every foll alt row K5, P133, K5.

Row 3 K6, [K5, bead 1, K6] 11 times, K5.

Row 5 K6, [K4, bead 1, K1, bead 1, K5] 11 times, K5.

Row 7 K6, *[K3, bead 1] twice, K4; rep from * to last 5 sts, K5.

Row 9 K6, *[K2, bead 1] 3 times, K3; rep from * to last 5 sts, K5.

Row 11 K6, *[K1, bead 1, K2, bead 1] twice, K2; rep from * to last 5 sts, K5.

Row 13 K6, *bead 1, K2, [bead 1, K1] twice, bead 1, K2, bead 1, K1; rep from * to last 5 sts, K5.

Row 15 K5, bead 1, *K2, [bead 1, K1] 3 times, bead 1, K2, bead 1; rep from * to last 5 sts, K5.

Row 17 K6, *[K1, bead 1] 5 times, K2; rep from * to last 5 sts, K5.

Row 19 As row 15.

Row 21 As row 13.

Row 23 As row 11.

Row 25 As row 9.

Row 27 As row 7.

Row 29 As row 5.

Row 31 As row 3.

Row 33 As row 5.

Row 35 K6, *K3, [bead 1, K1] twice, bead 1, K4; rep from * to last 5 sts, K5.

Row 37 K6, *K2, [bead 1, K1] 3 times, bead 1, K3; rep from * to last 5 sts, K5.

Row 39 As row 17.

Row 41 As row 37.

Row 43 As row 35.

Row 45 As row 5.

Row 47 As row 3.

Row 48 As row 2.

These 48 rows complete beaded border.

Break off yarn and remove beads.

Rejoin yarn and work lace section as follows:

Row 49 (RS) K6, *yfwd, sl 1, K1, psso, K1, K2tog, yfwd, K1; rep from * to last 5 sts, K5.

Row 50 and every foll alt row K5, P133, K5.

Row 51 K6, *yfwd, K1, sl 1, K2tog, psso, K1, yfwd, K1; rep from * to last 5 sts, K5.

Row 53 K6, *K2tog, yfwd, K1, yfwd, sl 1, K1, psso, K1; rep from * to last 5 sts, K5.

Row 55 K5, K2tog, *[K1, yfwd] twice, K1, sl 1, K2tog, psso; rep from * to last 10 sts, [K1, yfwd] twice, K1, sl 1, K1, psso, K5.

Row 57 K5, *K4, K2tog, yfwd, K1, yfwd, sl 1, K1, psso, K3; rep from * to last 6 sts, K6.

Row 58 As row 50.

Rep last 2 rows until Stole measures 140cm/55in, ending with RS facing for next row.

Next row As row 53.

Next and every foll alt row As row 50.

Next row As row 55.

Next row As row 49.

Next row As row 51.

Next row As row 50.

Break off yarn and thread on rem beads.

Rejoin yarn and work second beaded border as follows:

Work rows 31–46 as given for first beaded border, then work rows 3–32 as given for first beaded border.

Cast off very loosely.

MAKING UP

Press lightly on WS following instructions on yarn label and taking care not to damage beads.

Cut 260 lengths of yarn, each 30cm/12in long, and knot groups of 10 of these lengths through cast-on and cast-off edges to form fringe, positioning 13 knots evenly spaced along each end.

camisole

JENNIE ATKINSON

TO FIT BUST

97	102	107	112	117	122	cm
38	40	42	44	46	48	in

FINISHED MEASUREMENTS

Around bust

85	91	96	102	108	114	cm
33½	35¾	37¾	40	42½	45	in

(**Note:** Garment is designed to be very close fitting and to hug body tightly.)

Length to shoulder, including strap

55	56	57	58	59	60	cm
21½	22	22½	22¾	23¼	23½	in

YARN

4 (4: 5: 5: 5: 6) x 50g/1¾oz balls of Rowan *4-Ply Cotton* in Cream 153

NEEDLES

Pair of 2¾mm (UK no 12) (US size 2) knitting needles
Pair of 3mm (UK no 11) (US size 3) knitting needles

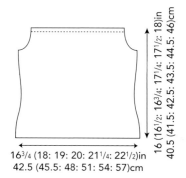

16¾ (18: 19: 20: 21¼: 22½)in
42.5 (45.5: 48: 51: 54: 57)cm

16 (16½: 16¾: 17¼: 17½: 18)in
40.5 (41.5: 42.5: 43.5: 44.5: 46)cm

TENSION

28 sts and 38 rows to 10cm/4in measured over st st using 3mm (US size 3) needles *or size to obtain correct tension.*

ABBREVIATIONS

See page 132.

BACK

Using 2¾mm (US size 2) needles, cast on 125 (133: 141: 149: 157: 165) sts.

Starting with a K row, work in st st for 7 rows, ending with WS facing for next row.

Change to 3mm (US size 3) needles.

Row 8 (WS) Purl.

Row 9 (picot foldline row) K1, *yfwd, K2tog; rep from * to end.

Work in st st for 9 rows more, ending with RS facing for next row.

Now place vertical lacy lines as follows:

Row 1 (RS) K35 (37: 39: 41: 43: 45), yfwd, sl 1, K1, psso, K25 (27: 29: 31: 33: 35), yfwd, K2tog, K24 (26: 28: 30: 32: 34), K2tog, yfwd, K to end.

Row 2 and every foll alt row Purl.

Row 3 As row 1.

Row 5 K2tog, K34 (36: 38: 40: 42: 44), yfwd, sl 1, K1, psso, K24 (26: 28: 30: 32: 34), yfwd, K2tog, K23 (25: 27: 29: 31: 33), K2tog, yfwd, K to last 2 sts, K2tog. 123 (131: 139: 147: 155: 163) sts.

Row 7 K35 (37: 39: 41: 43: 45), yfwd, sl 1, K1, psso, K24 (26: 28: 30: 32: 34), yfwd, K2tog, K23 (25: 27: 29: 31: 33), K2tog, yfwd, K to end.

Row 9 K2tog, K34 (36: 38: 40: 42: 44), yfwd, sl 1, K1, psso,

Row 2 P to last 5 sts, K5.

These 2 rows form patt for rest of Right Front.

Shape front slope, and underarm and sleeve seam

Next row (RS) K5, K2tog (for front slope decrease), patt to last st, inc in last st (for side seam increase).

Inc 1 st at side seam edge of next 43 rows, taking inc sts into patt and ending with RS facing for next row, **and at the same time** dec 1 st at front slope of 4th row and every foll 4th row, working all front slope decreases as set. 88 (92: 96: 100: 104: 108) sts.

Cast on 4 sts at beg of 2nd row and foll 4 (4: 5: 5: 6: 6) alt rows, then 60 (64: 66: 70: 70: 74) sts at beg of foll alt row, taking cast-on sts into patt, **and at the same time** dec 1 st at front slope edge of next row and 2 (2: 1: 2: 1: 0) foll 4th rows, then on 0 (0: 1: 0: 1: 2) foll 6th rows. 165 (173: 183: 191: 199: 207) sts.

Dec 1 st at front slope edge only on 2nd (4th: 4th: 2nd: 2nd: 4th) row and 1 (0: 0: 0: 0: 0) foll 4th row, then on every foll 6th row until 158 (166: 176: 183: 191: 199) sts rem.

Work straight until Right Front matches Backs to row worked on 6mm (US size 10) needle, ending with WS facing for next row.

Next row (WS) Using a 6mm (US size 10) needle, P to last 5 sts and slip these 153 (161: 171: 178: 186: 194) sts onto a holder, then using 4mm (US size 6) needles, K5. Work in garter st on these rem 5 sts (for back neck border extension) for 11 (11: 11: 11.5: 11.5: 11.5)cm/ 4¼ (4¼: 4¼: 4½: 4½: 4½)in, ending with RS facing for next row.

Cast off.

LEFT FRONT

Using 4mm (US size 6) needles, cast on 105 (109: 113: 117: 121: 125) sts.

Row 1 (RS) K13, [yfwd, K2tog, K21 (22: 23: 24: 25: 26) placing marker on 11th (12th: 12th: 13th: 13th: 14th) of these sts] twice, yfwd, K2tog, K19 (20: 21: 22: 23: 24) placing marker on 10th (11th: 11th: 12th: 12th: 13th) of these sts, yfwd, K2tog, K24 (25: 26: 27: 28: 29) placing marker on 10th (11th: 11th: 12th: 12th: 13th) of these sts.

Row 2 K5, P to end.

These 2 rows form patt – vertical lacy lines on a background of st st with front opening edge 5 sts in garter st. (There should be 4 marked sts – one between each pair of vertical lacy lines, and one between garter st

front border and first vertical lacy line.)

Work in patt for 8 rows more, ending with RS facing for next row.

Keeping vertical lacy lines correct as set, cont as follows:

Row 11 (RS) K1, K2tog, [patt to within 1 st of marked st, sl 1, K2tog (marked st is first of these 2 sts), psso] 4 times, patt to end. 96 (100: 104: 108: 112: 116) sts.

Work 9 rows.

Rep last 10 rows 3 times more, then row 11 again. 60 (64: 68: 72: 76: 80) sts.

Remove the 2 markers nearest front opening edge, leaving the 2 markers nearest side seam edge.

Work 7 rows, ending with RS facing for next row.

Row 59 (RS) Patt to last 9 sts and turn.

Row 60 Patt to end.

Row 61 K1, K2tog, [patt to within 1 st of marked st, sl 1, K2tog (marked st is first of these 2 sts), psso] twice, patt to last 13 sts and turn.

Remove last 2 markers – all decreases now complete.

There should now be a total of 55 (59: 63: 67: 71: 75) sts.

Row 62 Patt to end.

Row 63 Patt to last 17 sts and turn.

Row 64 Patt to end.

Row 65 Patt to last 21 sts and turn.

Row 66 Patt to end.

Row 67 Patt to last 25 sts and turn.

Row 68 Patt to end.

Row 69 Patt to last 29 sts and turn.

Row 70 Patt to end.

Cont in this way, working 4 fewer sts before turning on next row and every foll alt row, until the following row has been worked:

Row 79 (RS) Patt 6 (10: 14: 18: 22: 26) sts and turn.

Work 1 row across all sts.

Shape waist casing

Next row (RS) Knit.

Next row Knit.

Next row K5 (4: 3: 2: 1: 5), sl 1, K1, psso, yfwd, *K3, sl 1, K1, psso, yfwd; rep from * to last 8 sts, K8.

Next row Knit.

These 4 rows complete waist casing.

Now work in patt as follows:

Row 1 (RS) K6, *yfwd, K2tog, K9 (10: 11: 12: 13: 14); rep from * to last 5 sts, K5.

Row 2 K5, P to end.

These 2 rows form patt for rest of Left Front.

Shape front slope, and underarm and sleeve seam

Next row (RS) Inc in first st (for side seam increase), patt to last 7 sts, sl 1, K1, psso (for front slope decrease), K5. Inc 1 st at side seam edge of next 43 rows, taking inc sts into patt and ending with RS facing for next row, **and at the same time** dec 1 st at front slope of 4th row and every foll 4th row, working all front slope decreases as set. 88 (92: 96: 100: 104: 108) sts.

Cast on 4 sts at beg of next row and foll 4 (4: 5: 5: 6: 6) alt rows, then 60 (64: 66: 70: 70: 74) sts at beg of foll alt row, taking cast-on sts into patt, **and at the same time** dec 1 st at front slope edge of next row and 2 (2: 1: 2: 1: 0) foll 4th rows, then on 0 (0: 1: 0: 1: 2) foll 6th rows. 165 (173: 183: 191: 199: 207) sts.

Dec 1 st at front slope edge only on next (3rd: 3rd: next: next: 3rd) row and 1 (0: 0: 0: 0: 0) foll 4th row, then on every foll 6th row until 158 (166: 176: 183: 191: 199) sts rem.

Work straight until Left Front matches Backs to row worked on 6mm (US size 10) needle, ending with WS facing for next row.

Next row (WS) Using 4mm (US size 6) needles, K5, then using a 6mm (US size 10) needle, P to end and slip these 153 (161: 171: 178: 186: 194) sts onto a holder.

Break off yarn and rejoin it to rem 5 sts on needle. Work in garter st on these rem 5 sts (for back neck border extension) for 11 (11: 11: 11.5: 11.5: 11.5)cm/ 4¼ (4¼: 4¼: 4½: 4½: 4½)in, ending with RS facing for next row.

Cast off.

MAKING UP

Press lightly on WS following instructions on yarn label.

Join right overarm and shoulder seam

Holding RS of Right Front against RS of Right Back, rejoin yarn and using a 6mm (US size 10) needle, cast off first st of Right Front with first st of Right Back, cast off rem 152 (160: 170: 177: 185: 193) sts of Right Front with corresponding sts of Right Back, then cast off rem 27 (27: 27: 28: 28: 28) sts of Right Back.

Join left overarm and shoulder seam

Holding RS of Left Back against RS of Left Front, rejoin yarn and using a 6mm (US size 10) needle, cast off first st of Left Back with first st of Left Front, cast off rem 152 (160: 170: 177: 185: 193) sts of Left Back with corresponding sts of Left Front, then cast off rem 27 (27: 27: 28: 28: 28) sts of Left Back.

Sew centre back seam. Sew side and underarm sleeve seams. Sew together cast-off edges of back neck border extensions, then sew one edge to back neck cast-off sts.

Tie

Using double-pointed 4mm (US size 6) needles, cast on 4 sts.

Row 1 (RS) K4, without turning slip these 4 sts to opposite end of needle and bring yarn to opposite end of work pulling it quite tightly across WS of work ready to begin next row.

Rep row 1 until Tie is 183cm/72in long.

Cast off.

Thread Tie through eyelet holes of waist casing and tie ends at centre front.

PEPLUM JACKET

twisted rib cardigan

WENDY BAKER

TO FIT BUST

97	102	107	112	117	122	cm
38	40	42	44	46	48	in

FINISHED MEASUREMENTS

Around bust

121	125	130	135	139	144	cm
47½	49¼	51	53	54¾	56½	in

Length to shoulder

69	70	71	72	73	74	cm
27	27½	28	28¼	28¾	29	in

Sleeve seam

45	45	46	46	46	46	cm
17½	17½	18	18	18	18	in

YARN

17 (18: 19: 19: 20: 21) x 50g/1¾oz balls of Rowan *Wool Cotton* in Elf 946

NEEDLES

Pair of 4mm (UK no 8) (US size 6) knitting needles
Cable needle

EXTRAS

1 large decorative pin (or kilt pin) for fastening (optional)

TENSION

26 sts and 31 rows to 10cm/4in measured over patt using 4mm (US size 6) needles *or size to obtain correct tension.*

ABBREVIATIONS

See page 132.

SPECIAL ABBREVIATION

C3B = slip next 2 sts onto cable needle and leave at back of work, K1, then K2 from cable needle.

BACK

Using 4mm (US size 6) needles, cast on 157 (163: 169: 175: 181: 187) sts.
Row 1 (WS) K2 (5: 3: 1: 4: 2), P3, *K2, P3; rep from * to last 2 (5: 3: 1: 4: 2) sts, K2 (5: 3: 1: 4: 2).
Row 2 P2 (5: 3: 1: 4: 2), C3B, *P2, C3B; rep from * to last 2 (5: 3: 1: 4: 2) sts, P2 (5: 3: 1: 4: 2).
These 2 rows form patt.
Work straight in patt until Back measures 47 (47: 48: 48: 49: 49)cm/18½ (18½: 19: 19: 19¼: 19¼)in from cast-on edge, ending with RS facing for next row.
Shape armholes
Keeping patt correct, cast off 5 sts at beg of next 2 rows. 147 (153: 159: 165: 171: 177) sts.

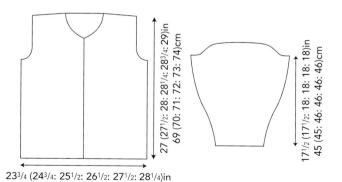

23¾ (24¾: 25½: 26½: 27½: 28¼)in
60.5 (62.5: 65: 67.5: 69.5: 72)cm

27 (27½: 28: 28¼: 28¾: 29)in
69 (70: 71: 72: 73: 74)cm

17½ (17½: 18: 18: 18: 18)in
45 (45: 46: 46: 46: 46)cm

Dec 1 st at each end of next row and foll 9 alt rows. 127 (133: 139: 145: 151: 157) sts.
Work straight until armhole measures 22 (23: 23: 24: 24: 25)cm/8½ (9: 9: 9½: 9½: 9¾)in, ending with RS facing for next row.

Shape shoulders
Cast off 13 (14: 15: 16: 17: 18) sts at beg of next 4 rows, then 14 (15: 16: 16: 17: 18) sts at beg of foll 2 rows. Cast off rem 47 (47: 47: 49: 49: 49) sts.

LEFT FRONT
Using 4mm (US size 6) needles, cast on 97 (100: 103: 106: 109: 112) sts.
Row 1 (WS) *K2, P3; rep from * to last 2 (5: 3: 1: 4: 2) sts, K2 (5: 3: 1: 4: 2).
Row 2 P2 (5: 3: 1: 4: 2), C3B, *P2, C3B; rep from * to last 2 sts, P2.
These 2 rows form patt.
Work straight in patt until Left Front matches Back to start of armhole shaping, ending with RS facing for next row.

Shape armhole
Keeping patt correct, cast off 5 sts at beg of next 2 rows. 92 (95: 98: 101: 104: 107) sts.
Work 1 row.
Dec 1 st at armhole edge of next row and foll 9 alt rows. 82 (85: 88: 91: 94: 97) sts.
Work straight until 23 rows fewer have been worked than on Back to start of shoulder shaping, ending with WS facing for next row.

Shape neck
Keeping patt correct, cast off 3 (3: 3: 4: 4: 4) sts at beg of next row, then 3 sts at beg of foll 11 alt rows, ending with RS facing for next row. 46 (49: 52: 54: 57: 60) sts.

Shape shoulder

Cast off 13 (14: 15: 16: 17: 18) sts at beg of next row,
then 3 sts at beg of foll row.
Rep last 2 rows once more.
Cast off rem 14 (15: 16: 16: 17: 18) sts.

RIGHT FRONT

Using 4mm (US size 6) needles, cast on 97 (100: 103:
106: 109: 112) sts.
Row 1 (WS) K2 (5: 3: 1: 4: 2), P3, *K2, P3; rep from * to
last 2 sts, K2.
Row 2 *P2, C3B; rep from * to last 2 (5: 3: 1: 4: 2) sts,
P2 (5: 3: 1: 4: 2).
These 2 rows form patt.
Complete to match Left Front, reversing shapings.

SLEEVES (make 2)

Using 4mm (US size 6) needles, cast on 72 (72: 74: 76:
76: 78) sts.
Row 1 (WS) P0 (0: 1: 2: 2: 3), *K2, P3; rep from * to last
2 (2: 3: 4: 4: 5) sts, K2, P0 (0: 1: 2: 2: 3).
Row 2 K0 (0: 1: 2: 2: 3), *P2, C3B; rep from * to last
2 (2: 3: 4: 4: 5) sts, P2, K0 (0: 1: 2: 2: 3).
These 2 rows form patt.
Work in patt until Sleeve measures 5cm/2in, ending with
RS facing for next row.
Inc 1 st at each end of next row and every foll 4th row to
110 (122: 114: 122: 122: 130) sts, then on every foll 6th
row until there are 122 (126: 126: 130: 130: 134) sts,
taking inc sts into patt.
Work straight until Sleeve measures 45 (45: 46: 46: 46:
46)cm/17½ (17½: 18: 18: 18: 18)in from cast-on edge,
ending with RS facing for next row.

Shape top

Keeping patt correct, cast off 5 sts at beg of next 2 rows.
112 (116: 116: 120: 120: 124) sts.
Dec 1 st at each end of next row and foll 8 alt rows, then
on foll row, ending with RS facing for next row.
Cast off rem 92 (96: 96: 100: 100: 104) sts.

MAKING UP

Press lightly on WS following instructions on yarn label.
Sew shoulder seams.

Collar

With RS facing and using 4mm (US size 6) needles,
starting and ending at front opening edges, pick up
and knit 48 (48: 48: 49: 49: 49) sts up right side of neck,
50 (50: 50: 52: 52: 52) sts from back, then 48 (48: 48: 49:
49: 49) sts down left side of neck. 146 (146: 146: 150:
150: 150) sts.
Row 1 (RS of Collar, WS of body) K10, *inc in next st,
K1, P2; rep from * to last 12 sts, inc in next st, K11.
178 (178: 178: 183: 183: 183) sts.
Row 2 Cast off 8 sts knitwise (one st on right needle
after cast-off), K1, *P3, K2; rep from * to last 8 sts, K8.
Row 3 Cast off 8 sts knitwise (one st on right needle
after cast-off), K1, *C3B, P2; rep from * to last 5 sts, C3B,
K2. 162 (162: 162: 167: 167: 167) sts.
Row 4 K2, *P3, K2; rep from * to end.
Row 5 K2, *C3B, P2; rep from * to last 5 sts, C3B, K2.
Rep last 2 rows until Collar measures 18cm/7in from pick-
up row, ending with WS of Collar facing for next row.
Cast off in patt.
Sew sleeves into armholes. Sew side and sleeve seams.
Fasten fronts with decorative pin if desired.

cabled bag

SHARON BRANT

SIZE

The finished bag measures 39cm/15½in wide at base by 35cm/13¾in tall.

YARN

3 x 100g/3½oz balls of Rowan *Scottish Tweed Aran* in Porridge 024

NEEDLES

Pair of 5mm (UK no 6) (US size 8) knitting needles
Cable needle

EXTRAS

Piece of stiff tieback interfacing, to insert inside bottom of bag (optional)

TENSION

16 sts and 24 rows to 10cm/4in measured over st st using 5mm (US size 8) needles *or size to obtain correct tension.*

ABBREVIATIONS

See page 132.

SPECIAL ABBREVIATION

C10F = slip next 5 sts onto cable needle and leave at front of work, K5, then K5 from cable needle.

FRONT OF BAG

Using 5mm (US size 8) needles, cast on 84 sts.
Note: The bag is worked in alternating vertical panels of st st cables and moss stitch, and markers are used to situate the beginning and end of each vertical panel.

Row 1 (RS) K1, [P1, K1] 6 times, place marker on right needle, *K10 for cable panel, place marker on right needle, [P1, K1] 7 times, place marker on right needle; rep from * once, K10 for cable panel, place marker on right needle, [K1, P1] 6 times, K1.
Row 2 K1, [P1, K1] 6 times, slip marker onto right needle, *P10 for cable panel, slip marker onto right needle, [P1, K1] 7 times, slip marker onto right needle; rep from * once, P10 for cable panel, slip marker onto right needle, [K1, P1] 6 times, K1.
These 2 rows set moss stitch and cable panels.
Slipping markers when reached and keeping moss st and cable panels correct as set, cont as follows:
Row 3 Moss st 13 sts, *K10, moss st 14 sts; rep from * once, K10, moss st 13 sts.
Row 4 Moss st 13 sts, *P10, moss st 14 sts; rep from * once, P10, moss st 13 sts.

Shape sides

Beg cables and shaping (at each side of each cable, within moss st panels) on next row as follows:
Row 5 Moss st to last 2 sts of first moss st panel, work 2 sts tog, *C10F across cable panel sts, work 2 sts tog, moss st to last 2 sts of this moss st panel, work 2 sts tog; rep from * once, C10F across cable panel, work 2 sts tog, moss st to end.
**Row 6 As row 4.
Rows 7–14 [Rep rows 3 and 4] 4 times.
Row 15 As row 5.** 72 sts.
Rep from ** to ** 5 times more. 42 sts.
Next row As row 4.
Next row As row 3.
Rep last 2 rows once more, ending with WS facing for next row.

Top border

Knit 3 rows.

Beg with a K row, work 8 rows in st st, ending with RS facing for next row.

Work holes for handles on next 2 rows as follows:

Next row (RS) P8, cast off 6 sts, P until there are 14 sts on needle after last cast-off, cast off 6 sts, P to end (this row forms hem foldline).

Next row Purl to end, casting on 6 sts over each group of 6 sts cast off on previous row.

Beg with a K row, work 8 rows in st st.

Cast off.

BACK OF BAG

Work exactly as for Front.

GUSSET

Using 5mm (US size 8) needles, cast on 20 sts.

Row 1 *K1, P1; rep from * to end.

Row 2 P1, K1; rep from * to end.

These 2 rows form moss st.

Work in moss st until Gusset is same length as cast-on edge of Front – this completes gusset at base of bag.

Shape first side panel of gusset

Mark each end of last row.

Next row (RS) Purl (to form a ridge at beg of side panel of gusset).

Beg with a P row, work in st st, dec 1 st at each end of 4th row and then every foll 6th row until 4 sts rem.

Work straight until Gusset measures from marker same as side edge of Front to top of cabled section, ending with WS facing for next row.

Knit 3 rows.

Cast off.

Shape second side panel of gusset

With RS facing and using 5mm (US size 8) needles, pick up and knit 20 sts along cast-on edge of gusset.

Next row (RS) Knit (to form a ridge at beg of side panel of gusset).

Beg with a K row, work in st st, dec 1 st at each end of 5th row and then every foll 6th row until 4 sts rem.

Work straight until Gusset measures from pick-up row same as side edge of Front to top of cabled section, ending with WS facing for next row.

Knit 3 rows. Cast off.

HANDLES (make 2)

Using 5mm (US size 8) needles, cast on 70 sts.

Knit 4 rows.

Cast off knitwise.

MAKING UP

Sew one side edge of Gusset to Front along two side edges and cast-on edge of Front, beginning and ending at top of garter st section at beg of border on Front. Then sew other side edge of Gusset to Back in same way. Insert about 3cm/1¼in of end of one Handle from RS to WS through a hole in hem on Front of bag, then slip stitch both sides of end of Handle to WS of top border. Insert other end of this Handle through other hole and stitch in place in same way.

Stitch second Handle to Back of bag in same way.

Fold hems on Front and Back to WS along foldline (level with holes) and slip stitch in place.

If desired, cut a piece of stiff tieback interfacing the same size as the bottom of the gusset (from cast-on edge to marker) and stitch in place inside bottom of bag.

CABLED BAG

knitting information

The following notes will help you produce successful knitted garments.

TENSION

Obtaining the correct tension can make the difference between a garment that fits and one that does not. It controls both the shape and size of a knitted garment, so any variation, however slight, can distort the finished size. Different designers feature in this book and it is their tension, given at the start of each pattern, that you must match. To check this against your own tension, knit a square in pattern and/or stocking stitch (depending on the pattern instructions) of about 5 to 10 more stitches and 5 to 10 more rows than those given in the tension note. Mark a central 10cm (4in) square with pins. If you have too many stitches to 10cm (4in), try again using a larger needle size. If you have too few stitches to 10cm (4in), try again using a smaller needle size.

Once you have achieved the correct tension, your garment will be knitted to the measurements indicated in the size diagram shown with the pattern.

GARMENT SIZES AND SIZE DIAGRAMS

The instructions in each garment pattern are given for the smallest size. The figures in parentheses are for the larger sizes. Where there is one set of figures only, it applies to all sizes.

All garment patterns include 'ease' to allow for a comfortable fit. The finished measurement around the bust of the knitted garment is given at the start of each pattern and includes this ease. The size diagram shows the finished width of the garment at the underarm, and it is this measurement that you should use to choose an appropriate size.

A useful tip is to measure one of your own garments that fits comfortably and choose a size that is similar. Having chosen a size based on width, look at the corresponding length for that size; if you are not happy with the total length that we recommend, adjust your own garment before beginning your armhole shaping – any adjustment after this point will mean that your sleeve will not fit into your garment easily; and don't forget to take your adjustment into account if there is any side-seam shaping.

Finally, look at the sleeve length; the size diagram shows the finished sleeve measurement, taking into account any top-arm insertion length. Measure your body between the centre of your neck and your wrist, this measurement should correspond to half the garment width plus the sleeve length. Again, your sleeve length may be adjusted, but remember to take into consideration the position of the sleeve increases if you do adjust the length. (See pages 6–13 for more about making alterations.)

KNITTING CHARTS

Two of the patterns in the book have charts as part of the instructions. Each square on a knitting chart represents a stitch and each line of squares represents a row of knitting. The key with the chart explains the symbols used on the chart.

When working from the charts, read odd-numbered rows (K) from right to left and even-numbered rows (P) from left to right, unless stated otherwise.

COLOURWORK KNITTING

There are two main methods of working colour into a knitted fabric: the intarsia and Fair Isle techniques. The first method produces a single thickness of fabric and is usually used where a colour is only required in a particular area of a row. Where a repeating pattern is created across the row, the Fair Isle technique is usually used.

Intarsia technique

For this technique, cut lengths of yarn for each motif or block of colour used in a row. Then join in the various colours at the appropriate position in the row, linking one colour to the next by twisting them around each other where they meet on the wrong side to avoid gaps.

All yarn ends can then either be darned along the colour join lines after each motif is completed, or can be 'knitted-in' on the wrong side of the knitting as each colour is worked into the pattern. This is done in much the same way as 'weaving-in' yarns when working the Fair Isle technique and saves time darning-in ends.

It is essential that the tension is noted for colourwork, because this may vary from the plain stocking stitch tension if both are used in the same pattern.

Fair Isle technique

When two or three colours are worked repeatedly across a row, strand the yarn not in use loosely behind the stitches being worked. If you are working with more than two colours, treat the 'floating' yarns as if they were one yarn and always spread the stitches to their correct width to keep them elastic.

It is advisable not to carry the stranded or 'floating' yarns over more than three stitches at a time, but to weave them under and over the colour you are working to catch the 'floating' yarns into the back of the work.

SLIP-STITCH EDGINGS

When a row end edge forms the actual finished edge of a garment or an accessory like a scarf, a slip-stitch edging makes a neat edge.

To work a slip-stitch edging at the end of a right-side row, work across the row until there is one stitch left on the left needle. Pick up the loop lying between the needles and place this loop on the right needle. (Note that this loop does NOT count as a stitch and is not included in any stitch counts.) Now slip the last stitch knitwise with the yarn at the back of the work. At the beginning of the next row, purl together the first (slipped) stitch with the picked-up loop.

To work a slip-stitch edging at the end of a wrong-side row, work across the row until there is one stitch left on the left needle. Pick up the loop lying between the needles and place this loop on the right needle. (Note that this loop does NOT count as a stitch and is not included in any stitch counts.) Now slip the last stitch purlwise with the yarn at the front of the work. At the beginning of the next row, knit together through the back of the loop the first (slipped) stitch with the picked-up loop.

FINISHING INSTRUCTIONS

Follow these finishing tips for a truly professional-looking garment or accessory.

Blocking and pressing

Block out each piece of knitting by pinning it to the correct size on a padded surface. Following the instructions on the yarn label and avoiding any ribbing, press the pieces.

Take special care to press the edges, as this will make sewing the seams both easier and neater. If the yarn label indicates that the fabric should not be pressed, then covering the blocked out fabric with a damp white cotton cloth and leaving it to dry will have the desired effect.

Darn in all ends neatly along the selvage edge or a colour join, as appropriate.

Sewing seams

When sewing the pieces together, remember to match areas of colour and texture very carefully where they meet. Use backstitch or mattress stitch for all main knitting seams, and sew together ribbing and neckband seams with mattress stitch, unless stated otherwise.

Having completed the garment pieces, sew the seams in the order stated in the instructions. After sewing the shoulder seams, sew the top of the sleeve to the body of the garment using the method detailed in the pattern, referring to the appropriate guide:

Straight cast-off sleeves Place the centre of the cast-off edge of the sleeve at the shoulder seam. Sew the top of the sleeve to the back and front.

Square set-in sleeves Place the centre of the cast-off edge of the sleeve at the shoulder seam. Sew the top of the sleeve into the armhole, with the straight sides at the top of the sleeve forming a neat right-angle to the cast-off stitches at the armhole.

Shallow set-in sleeves Place the centre of the cast-off edge of the sleeve at the shoulder seam. Match the decreases at the beginning of the armhole shaping with the decreases at the top of the sleeve, and sew the sleeve head to the armhole, easing in the shapings.

Set-in sleeves Place the centre of the cast-off edge of the sleeve at the shoulder seam. Sew in the sleeve, easing the sleeve head into the armhole.

Lastly, slip stitch any pocket edgings and linings in place and sew on buttons to correspond with buttonholes.

KNITTING ABBREVIATIONS

The following are the standard knitting abbreviations used in this book. Any special abbreviations (such as those for cables or beading) are given at the beginning of individual patterns.

alt	alternate
beg	begin(ning)
cm	centimetre(s)
cont	continu(e)(ing)
dec	decreas(e)(ing)
DK	double knitting (a lightweight yarn)
foll	follow(s)(ing)
g	gram(s)
garter st	garter stitch (K every row)
in	inch(es)
inc	increas(e)(ing)
inc 1	increase one st by working into front and back of stitch
K	knit
K2tog	knit next 2 sts together
m	metre(s)
M1	make one stitch by picking up horizontal loop before next stitch and knitting into back of it
MC	main colour (of yarn)
mm	millimetre(s)
oz	ounce(s)
P	purl
P2tog	purl next 2 sts together
patt	pattern; or work in pattern
psso	pass slipped stitch over

rem	remain(s)(ing)
rep	repeat(s)(ing)
rev st st	reverse stocking stitch (P all RS rows and K all WS rows)
RS	right side
sl	slip
st(s)	stitch(es)
st st	stocking stitch (K all RS rows and P all WS rows)
tbl	through back of loop(s)
tog	together
WS	wrong side
yd	yard(s)
yfrn	yarn forward (between needles) and round right needle to make a new stitch
yfwd	yarn forward (between needles) and over right needle to make a new stitch
yon	yarn over right needle to make a new stitch
yrn	yarn round right needle to make a new stitch

0	no stitches, times or rows for that size
–	instructions do not apply to this size
*	Repeat instructions after asterisk or between asterisks as many times as instructed.
[ ]	Repeat instructions inside square brackets as many times as instructed.

The following are the specifications of the Rowan yarns used for the designs in this book (see page 134 for yarn weight symbols). It is always best to try to obtain the exact yarns specified in the patterns. If, however, you wish to find a substitute yarn, use the yarn descriptions given below to find a similar yarn type and yarn weight. When substituting yarn, remember to calculate the yarn amount needed by metrage/yardage rather than by ball weight.

For yarn care directions, refer to the yarn label.

Rowan Classic Baby Alpaca DK

A lightweight alpaca yarn; 100 per cent baby alpaca; 50g/1³/₄oz (approximately 100m/109yd) per ball; recommended tension – 22 sts and 30 rows to 10cm/4in measured over st st using 4mm (US size 6) knitting needles.

Rowan Classic Cashsoft 4-Ply

A super-fine-weight wool-and-cashmere-mix yarn; 57 per cent fine merino wool, 33 per cent microfibre, 10 per cent cashmere; 50g/1³/₄oz (approximately 180m/197yd) per ball; recommended tension – 28 sts and 36 rows to 10cm/4in measured over st st using 3¹/₄mm (US size 3) knitting needles.

Rowan Classic Silk Wool DK

A lightweight wool-and-silk-mix yarn; 50 per cent silk, 50 per cent merino wool; 50g/1³/₄oz (approximately 100m/109yd) per ball; recommended tension – 22 sts and 30 rows to 10cm/4in measured over st st using 4mm (US size 6) knitting needles.

Rowan Cotton Glace

A fine-weight cotton yarn; 100 per cent cotton; 50g/1³/₄oz (approximately 115m/126yd) per ball; recommended tension – 23 sts and 32 rows to 10cm/4in measured over st st using 3¹/₄–3³/₄mm (US sizes 3–5) knitting needles.

Rowan Denim

A lightweight cotton yarn; 100 per cent cotton;

50g/1³/₄oz (approximately 93m/102yd) per ball; recommended tension – 20 sts and 28 rows (before washing) and 20 sts and 32 rows (after washing) to 10cm/4in measured over st st using 4mm (US size 6) knitting needles.

Rowan 4-Ply Cotton

A super-fine-weight cotton yarn; 100 per cent cotton; 50g/1³/₄oz (approximately 170m/186yd) per ball; recommended tension – 27–29 sts and 37–39 rows to 10cm/4in measured over st st using 3mm (US size 3) knitting needles.

Rowan Kidsilk Haze

A fine-weight mohair-mix yarn; 70 per cent super kid mohair, 30 per cent silk; 25g/⁷/₈oz (approximately 210m/229yd) per ball; recommended tension – 18–25 sts and 23–34 rows to 10cm/4in measured over st st using 3¹/₄–5mm (US sizes 3–8) knitting needles.

Rowan Scottish Tweed Aran

A medium-weight wool yarn; 100 per cent pure wool; 100g/3¹/₂oz (approximately 170m/186yd) per ball; recommended tension – 16 sts and 23 rows to 10cm/4in measured over st st using 5–5¹/₂mm (US sizes 8–9) knitting needles.

Rowan Scottish Tweed DK

A lightweight wool yarn; 100 per cent pure wool; 50g/1³/₄oz (approximately 113m/123yd) per ball; recommended tension – 20–22 sts and 28–30 rows to 10cm/4in measured over st st using 4mm (US size 6) knitting needles.

Rowan Wool Cotton

A lightweight wool/cotton blend yarn; 50 per cent merino wool, 50 per cent cotton; 50g/1³/₄oz (approximately 113m/123yd) per ball; recommended tension – 22–24 sts and 30–32 rows to 10cm/4in measured over st st using 3³/₄–4mm (US size 5–6) knitting needles.

Categories of yarn, tension ranges, and recommended knitting needle sizes from the Craft Yarn Council of America.
YarnStandards.com

Yarn-weight symbol and category names	0 LACE	1 SUPER FINE	2 FINE	3 LIGHT	4 MEDIUM	5 BULKY	6 SUPER BULKY
Types of yarns** in category	No.10 crochet cotton, fingering	4-ply, sock, fingering, baby	sport, baby	DK, light worsted	Aran, worsted, afghan	chunky, craft, rug	bulky, roving
Knit tension ranges* in st st to 10cm (4in)	33–40*** sts	27–32 sts	23–26 sts	21–24 sts	16–20 sts	12–15 sts	6–11 sts
Recommended needle in metric size range	1.5–2.25 mm	2.25–3.25 mm	3.25–3.75 mm	3.7.5–4.5 mm	4.5–5.5 mm	6.5–8 mm	8mm and larger
Recommended needle in US size range	000 to 1	1 to 3	3 to 5	5 to 7	7 to 9	9 to 11	11 and larger

* **GUIDELINES ONLY** The above reflect the most commonly used tensions and needle sizes for specific yarn categories.
** The generic yarn-weight names in the yarn categories include those commonly used in the UK and US.

*** Ultra-fine lace-weight yarns are difficult to put into tension ranges; always follow the tension given in your pattern for these yarns.

Contact the distributors listed here to find a supplier of Rowan hand knitting yarns near you. For countries not listed, contact the main office in the UK or the Rowan websites:

www.knitrowan.com
www.rowanclassic.com

UK
Rowan, Green Lane Mill, Holmfirth, West Yorkshire HD9 2DX, England.
Tel: +44 (0) 1484 681881.
Fax: +44 (0) 1484 687920.
E-mail: mail@knitrowan.com

AUSTRALIA
Australian Country Spinners, 314 Albert Street, Brunswick, Victoria 3056. Tel: (61) 3 9380 3888.
Fax: (61) 3 9387 2674.
E-mail: sales@auspinners.com.au

AUSTRIA
Coats Harlander GmbH, Autokaderstrasse 31, A-1230 Wien.
Tel: (01) 27716-0.
Fax: (01) 27716-228.

BELGIUM
Coats Benelux, Ring Oost 14A, Ninove, 9400.
Tel: 0346 35 37 00.
E-mail: sales.coatsninove@coats.com

CANADA
Same as USA.

CHINA
Coats Shanghai Ltd., No. 9 Building, Boasheng Road, Songjiang Industrial Zone, Shanghai, 201613.
Tel: (86-21) 5774 3733.
Fax: (86-21) 5774 3768.

DENMARK
Coats HP A/S, Nannagade 28, 2200 Kobenhavn N.
Tel: 35 86 90 50. Fax: 35 82 15 10.
E-mail: info@hpgruppen.dk
www.hpgruppen.dk

FINLAND
Coats Opti Oy, Ketjutie 3, 04220 Kerava. Tel: (358) 9 274 871.
Fax: (358) 9 2748 7330.
E-mail: coatsopti.sales@coats.com

FRANCE
Coats France/Steiner Fréres, SAS 100 avenue du Général de Gaulle, 18 500 Mehun-Sur-Yèvre.
Tel: 02 48 23 12 30.
Fax: 02 48 23 12 40.

GERMANY
Coats GMbH, Kaiserstrasse 1, D-79341 Kenzingen.
Tel: 7644 8020. Fax: 7644 802399.
www.coatsgmbh.de

HOLLAND
Same as Belgium.

HONG KONG
Coats China Holding Ltd., 19/F Millenium City 2, 378 Kwun Tong Road, Kwun Tong, Kowloon.
Tel: (852) 2798 6886.
Fax: (852) 2305 0311.

ICELAND
Storkurinn, Laugavegi 59, 101 Reykjavek. Tel: (354) 551 8258.
E-mail: storkurinn@simnet.is

ITALY
Coats Cucirini srl, Via Sarca 223, 20126 Milano.
Tel: 800 992377.

Fax: 0266111701.
E-mail: servizio.clienti@coats.com

JAPAN
Puppy-Jardin Co. Ltd., 3-8 11 Kudanminami, Chiyodaku, Hiei Kudan Bldg. 5F, Tokyo.
Tel: (81) 3 3222-7076.
Fax: (81) 3 3222-7066.
E-mail: info@rowan-jaeger.com

KOREA
Coats Korea Co. Ltd., 5F Kuckdong B/D, 935-40 Bangbae-Dong, Seocho-Gu, Seoul.
Tel: (82) 2 521 6262.
Fax: (82) 2 521 5181.

LEBANON
y.knot, Saifi Village, Mkhalissiya Street 162, Beirut.
Tel: (961) 1 992211.
Fax: (961) 1 315553.
E-mail: yknot@cyberia.net.lb

LUXEMBERG
Same as Belgium.

MEXICO
Estambres Crochet SA de CV, Aaron Saenz 1891-7, Monterrey, NL 64650.
Tel: +52 (81) 8335-3870.

NEW ZEALAND
ACS New Zealand, 1 March Place, Belfast, Christchurch.
Tel: 64-3-323-6665.
Fax: 64-3-323-6660.

NORWAY
Coats Knappehuset AS, Pb 100 Ulset, 5873 Bergen.
Tel: (47) 55 53 93 00.
Fax: (47) 55 53 93 93.

PORTUGAL
Apartado 444, 4431958 Vila Nova
de Gaia. Tel: (351) 2237 70773.
Fax: (351) 2237 70705.
E-mail: elvira.castro@coats.com

SINGAPORE
Golden Dragon Store,
101 Upper Cross Street #02-51,
People's Park Centre, Singapore
058357. Tel: (65) 6 5358454.
Fax: (65) 6 2216278.
E-mail: gdscraft@hotmail.com

SOUTH AFRICA
Arthur Bales PTY, P.O. BOX 44644,
62 4th Avenue, Linden 2104.
Tel: (27) 11 888 2401.
Fax: (27) 11 782 6137.

SPAIN
Oyambre, Pau Claris 145,
80009 Barcelona.
Tel: (34) 670 011957.
Fax: (34) 93 4872672.

E-mail: oyambre@oyambreonline.com
Coats Fabra, Santa Adria 20,
08030 Barcelona.
Tel: 93 2908400. Fax: 93 2908409.
E-mail: atencion.clientes@coats.com

SWEDEN
Coats Expotex AB, Division Craft,
Box 297, 401 24 Göteborg.
Tel: (46) 33 720 79 00.
Fax: (46) 31 47 16 50.

SWITZERLAND
Coats Stroppel AG, Stroppelstrasse
16, CH-5300 Tungi (AG).
Tel: 056 298 12 20.
Fax: 056 298 12 50.

TAIWAN
Cactus Quality Co. Ltd., P.O. Box 30
485, Taipei.
Office: 7Fl-2, No 140, Roosevelt
Road, Sec 2, Taipei.
Tel: 886-2-23656527.
Fax: 886-2-23656503.
E-mail: cqcl@m17.hinet.net

THAILAND
Global Wide Trading,
10 Lad Prao Soi 88, Bangkok 10310.
Tel: 00 662 933 9019.
Fax: 00 662 933 9110.
E-mail: theneedleworld@yahoo.com

USA
Westminster Fibers Inc.,
165 Ledge Street, Nashua,
NH 03060.
Tel: 1-800-445-9276.
E-mail: rowan@westminsterfibers.com
www.westminsterfibers.com

author's acknowledgments

I would like to take the opportunity to thank the following: Kate Buller of Rowan yarns for the opportunity to do this book; all the designers for their wonderful designs; the team of editors, designer, photographer and stylists who put the book together so beautifully; Penny Hill for her skill and her lovely knitters; Joy, Ruby and Mary for knitting for me; Sue Whiting and Emma King for pattern writing and checking respectively; and, last but not least, Mum for her invaluable help in finishing off garments and Dad for aving a much needed glass of wine on the table for me!